Book of Shadows for Coloring

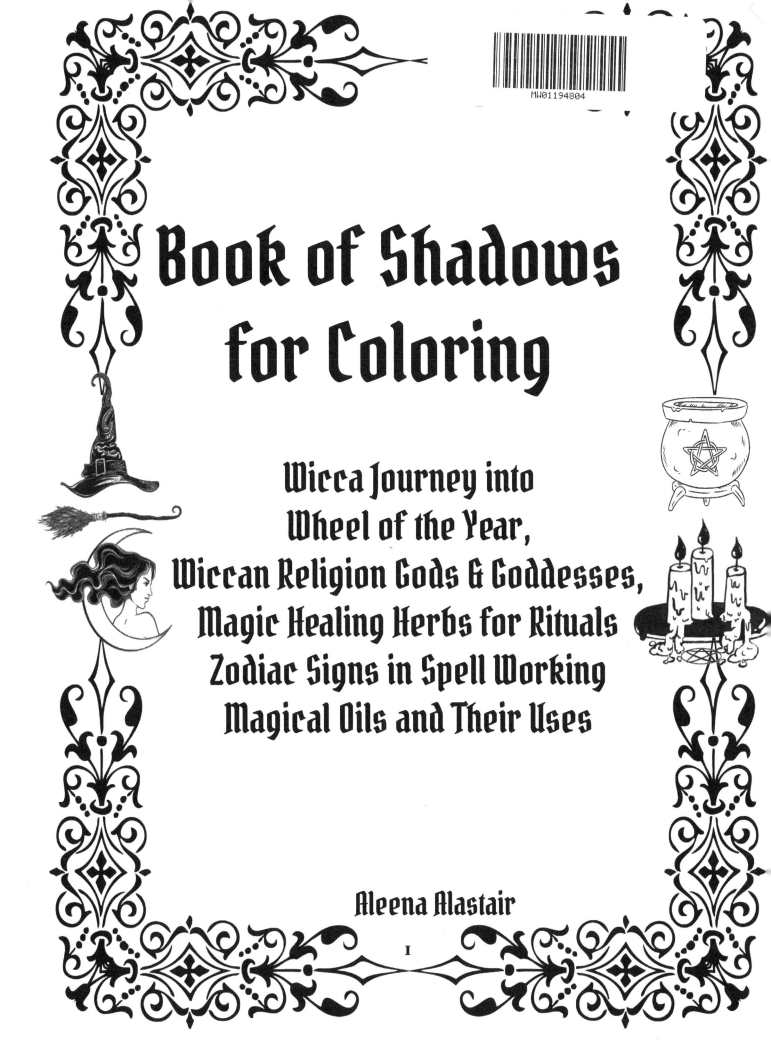

**Wicca Journey into
Wheel of the Year,
Wiccan Religion Gods & Goddesses,
Magic Healing Herbs for Rituals
Zodiac Signs in Spell Working
Magical Oils and Their Uses**

Aleena Alastair

Flip Through:

Wicca Journey into Wheel of the year, Gods, Herbs, Incenses, Zodiac, and Oils

COLORING BOOK OF SHADOWS

http://bit.ly/Vol0BOS

Copyright 2017 by Aleena Alastair
Publisher: Witchcraft & Wicca
Website: https://witchcraft-wicca.com
ISBN: 9781545000571

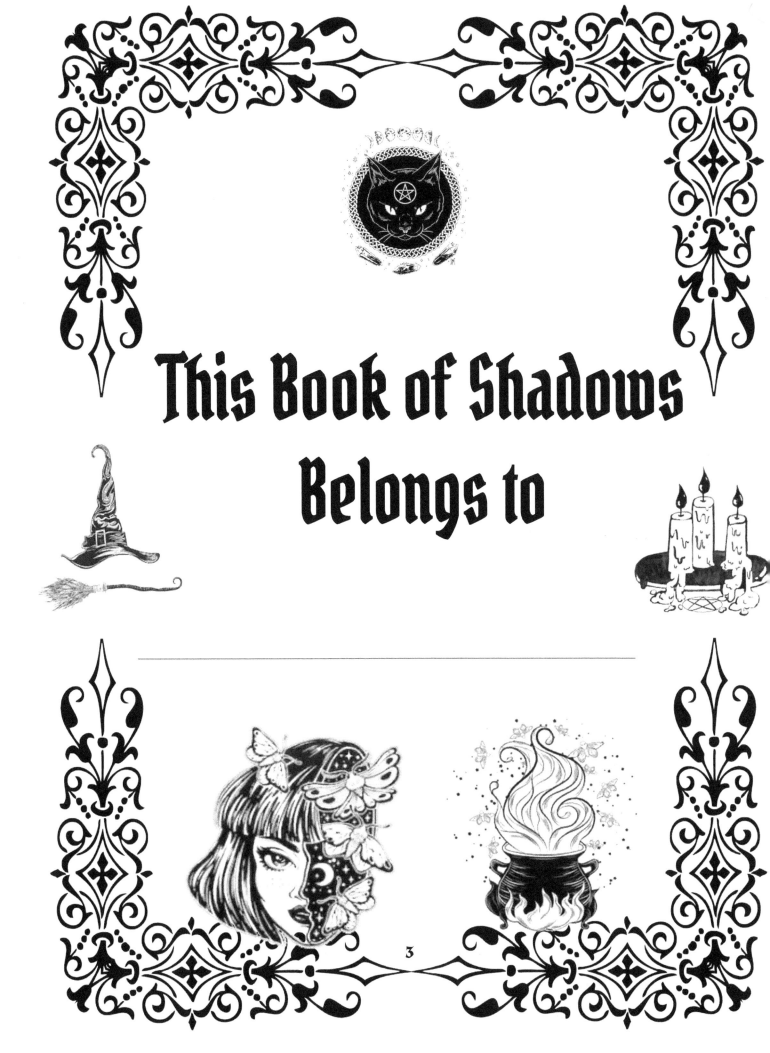

This Book of Shadows
Belongs to

Signs of a Spell Working

My Feelings & Emotions

Coincidences:

Dreams:

New Opportunities:

Indirect Indicators:

Increased Contact:

Chapter 1

The Wheel
of the Year

Notes for Chapter 1

Yule

December 21st.

Symbols of Yule

You may wish to use some of the following items to decorate your altar or your home or to plan a ritual for this holiday.

Incense: Bayberry, Cedar, Cinnamon, Frankincense, Ginger, Juniper, Myrrh, Pine, Sage, Spruce

Colors: Gold, Green, Red, Silver, White

Stones: Alexandrite, Bloodstone, Blue Topaz, Citrine, Clear Quartz, Diamond, Emerald, Garnet, Green Tourmaline, Kunzite, Jet, Pearl, Rubies, Tiger's Eye

Herbs: Bayberry, Birch, Blessed thistle, Chamomile, Cinnamon, Comfrey, Elder, Evergreen, Fir, Frankincense, Hazel Bark, Holly, Ivy, Mistletoe, Oak, Pine, Rosemary, Sage, Yellow Cedar, Wintergreen

Symbols: Bells, Candles, Clove, Evergreens, Holly, Mistletoe, Snowflake, Wreath

Food: Ale, Caraway Cakes, Cookies, Eggnog, Fruits, Ginger tea, Gingerbread, Nutmeg, Nuts, Pork dishes, Roast apples, Spiced cider, Sugar, Turkey, Wassail

Gods and Goddesses: Apollo, Attis, Balder, Bacchus, Dionysus, The Green Man, Helios, Lugh, The Oak King, Odin, Ra, Sol

Wiccan Sabbats
Rituals & Spells

Purpose:

Ingredients

When?

How?

Variations

Notes

My Altar and Sabbat Shrine

Sabbat Recipes

Imbolc

February 1st.

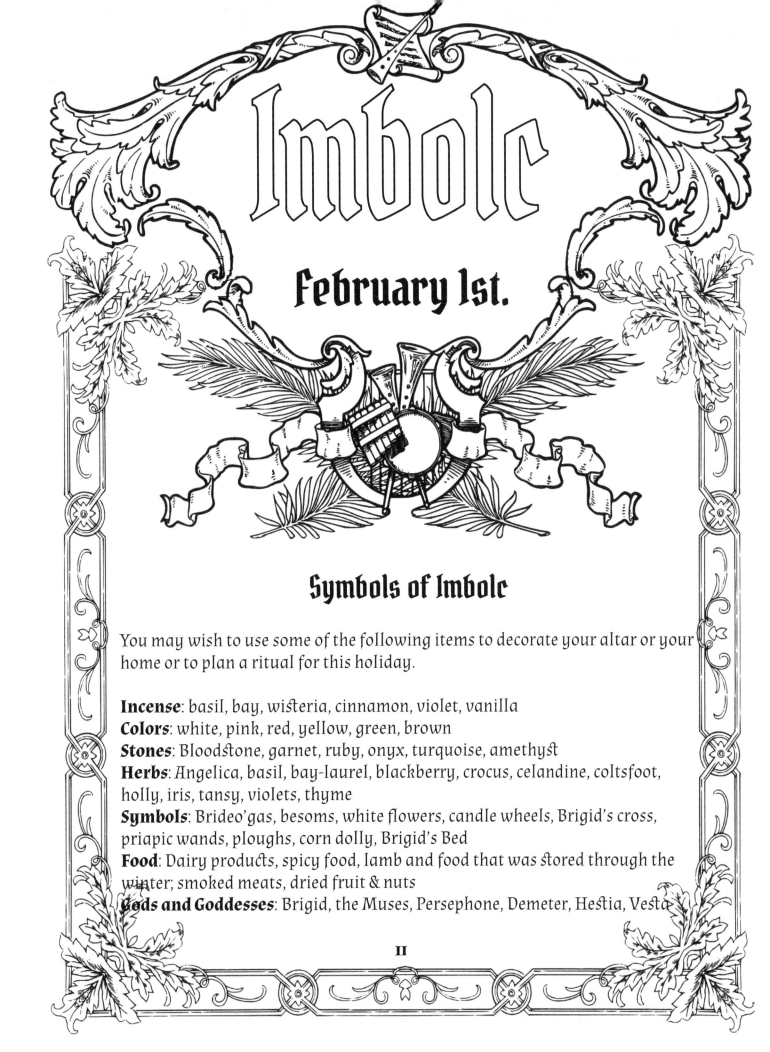

Symbols of Imbolc

You may wish to use some of the following items to decorate your altar or your home or to plan a ritual for this holiday.

Incense: basil, bay, wisteria, cinnamon, violet, vanilla
Colors: white, pink, red, yellow, green, brown
Stones: Bloodstone, garnet, ruby, onyx, turquoise, amethyst
Herbs: Angelica, basil, bay-laurel, blackberry, crocus, celandine, coltsfoot, holly, iris, tansy, violets, thyme
Symbols: Brideo'gas, besoms, white flowers, candle wheels, Brigid's cross, priapic wands, ploughs, corn dolly, Brigid's Bed
Food: Dairy products, spicy food, lamb and food that was stored through the winter; smoked meats, dried fruit & nuts
Gods and Goddesses: Brigid, the Muses, Persephone, Demeter, Hestia, Vesta

Wiccan Sabbats Rituals & Spells

Purpose:

Ingredients

When?

How?

Variations

Notes

My Altar and Sabbat Shrine

Sabbat Recipes

Ostara

March 21st.

Symbols of Ostara

You may wish to use some of the following items to decorate your altar or your home or to plan a ritual for this holiday.

Incense: Floral of any type. Jasmine, African violet, rose, sage, strawberry, violet flowers, orange peel, rose petals, lotus, magnolia, ginger.

Colours: All pastels, yellow, pink, green, blue

Stones: Rose quartz, aquamarine, amethyst, jasper and moonstone.

Flowers And Herbs: all spring flowers. Irish moss, crocus flowers, daffodils, Easter lilies, roses, strawberry, acorn, celandine, dandelion, dogwood, honeysuckle, iris, jasmine, rose, tansy, violet

Symbols: Colored eggs, seeds, earth, flowers and herbs

Foods: Eggs, honey, bread, seeds, sprouts and green leafy vegetables

Gods: Gods of Love, Moon Gods, Gods of Song & Dance, some Fertility Gods. Some Ostara Gods are Adonis, Lord of the Greenwood, Ovis, Dylan, Odin, Osiris, Attis, Mithras.

Goddesses: Virgin Goddesses, Moon Goddesses, Goddesses of Love, Androgynous Deities, some Fertility Goddesses. Some Ostara Goddesses are Aphrodite, Eostre, Ma-Ku, Lady of the Lake, Minerva, Isis, Rheda, Coatlique.

Wiccan Sabbats Rituals & Spells

Purpose:

Ingredients

When?

How?

Variations

Notes

My Altar and Sabbat Shrine

Sabbat Recipes

Beltane

May 1st.

Symbols of Beltane

You may wish to use some of the following items to decorate your altar or your home or to plan a ritual for this holiday.

Incense- Frankincense, lilac, rose, musk, ylang ylang, tuberose, jasmine
Colors- green, pink, blue, yellow
Stones- rose quartz, beryl, garnet
Herbs– Honeysuckle, St John's Wort, hawthorn, phlox, rose, lilac, all flowers
Symbols- May pole, wreaths of flowers, strings of beads, ribbons, phallic symbols, cauldron
Food- Dairy, oatcakes, cherry, strawberry, May wine, salad greens
Gods and Goddesses: Bel, Belanos, Aphrodite, Adonis, Achilles, Arianhrod, Ariel, Artemis, Astarte, Anghus Og, Cybele, Diana, Freya, Rhiannon, Shiela-na-gig, Skadi, Var, Venus, Xochiquetzal, Apollo, Bacchus, Cernnunos, Cupid, Eros, Faunus, Frey, the Horned God, Herne, Odin, Orion, Pan, Puck, Robin Goodfellow, Maia

Wiccan Sabbats
Rituals & Spells

Purpose:

Ingredients

When?

How?

Variations

Notes

20

My Altar and Sabbat Shrine

Sabbat Recipes

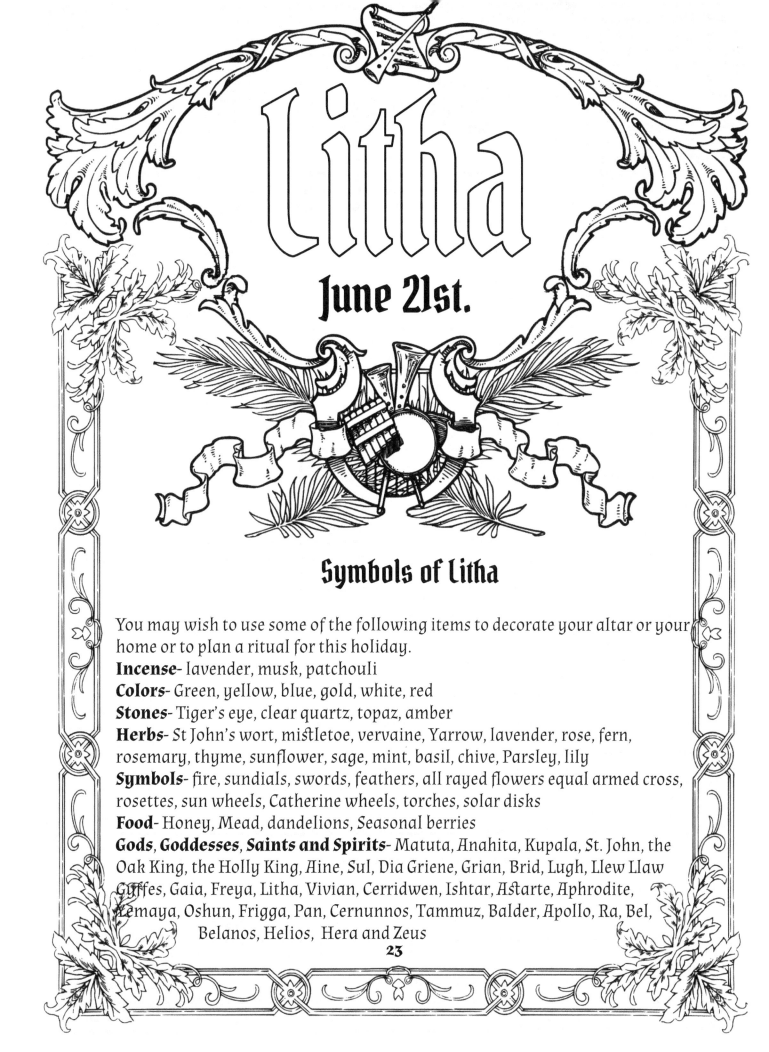

Litha

June 21st.

Symbols of Litha

You may wish to use some of the following items to decorate your altar or your home or to plan a ritual for this holiday.

Incense- lavender, musk, patchouli

Colors- Green, yellow, blue, gold, white, red

Stones- Tiger's eye, clear quartz, topaz, amber

Herbs- St John's wort, mistletoe, vervaine, Yarrow, lavender, rose, fern, rosemary, thyme, sunflower, sage, mint, basil, chive, Parsley, lily

Symbols- fire, sundials, swords, feathers, all rayed flowers equal armed cross, rosettes, sun wheels, Catherine wheels, torches, solar disks

Food- Honey, Mead, dandelions, Seasonal berries

Gods, Goddesses, Saints and Spirits- Matuta, Anahita, Kupala, St. John, the Oak King, the Holly King, Aine, Sul, Dia Griene, Grian, Brid, Lugh, Llew Llaw Gyffes, Gaia, Freya, Litha, Vivian, Cerridwen, Ishtar, Astarte, Aphrodite, Yemaya, Oshun, Frigga, Pan, Cernunnos, Tammuz, Balder, Apollo, Ra, Bel, Belanos, Helios, Hera and Zeus

Wiccan Sabbats
Rituals & Spells

Purpose:

Ingredients

When?

How?

Variations

Notes

My Altar and Sabbat Shrine

Sabbat Recipes

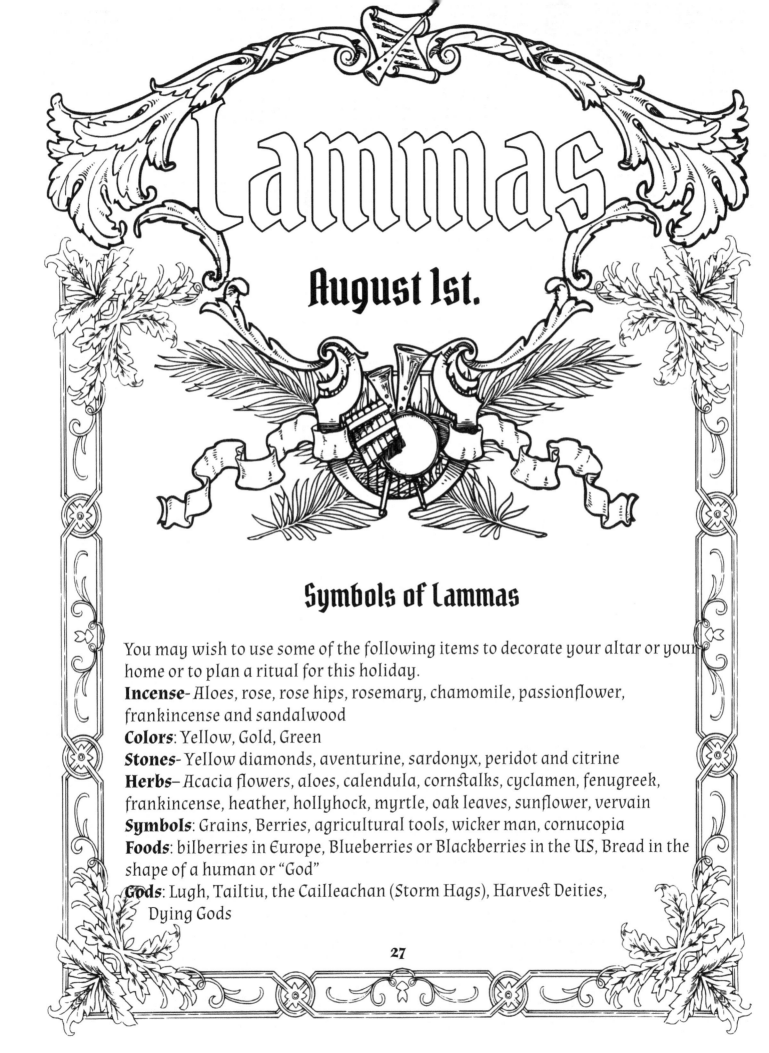

Lammas

August 1st.

Symbols of Lammas

You may wish to use some of the following items to decorate your altar or your home or to plan a ritual for this holiday.

Incense- Aloes, rose, rose hips, rosemary, chamomile, passionflower, frankincense and sandalwood

Colors: Yellow, Gold, Green

Stones- Yellow diamonds, aventurine, sardonyx, peridot and citrine

Herbs- Acacia flowers, aloes, calendula, cornstalks, cyclamen, fenugreek, frankincense, heather, hollyhock, myrtle, oak leaves, sunflower, vervain

Symbols: Grains, Berries, agricultural tools, wicker man, cornucopia

Foods: bilberries in Europe, Blueberries or Blackberries in the US, Bread in the shape of a human or "God"

Gods: Lugh, Tailtiu, the Cailleachan (Storm Hags), Harvest Deities, Dying Gods

Wiccan Sabbats Rituals & Spells

Purpose:

Ingredients

When?

How?

Variations

Notes

My Altar and Sabbat Shrine

Sabbat Recipes

Mabon

September 21st.

Symbols of Mabon

You may wish to use some of the following items to decorate your altar or your home or to plan a ritual for this holiday.

Incense - Benzoin, Cedar, Frankincense, Myrrh, Pine

Colors - Brown, Red, Maroon, Orange, Yellow, Gold,

Stones - Amber, Amethyst, Citrine, Topaz, Tiger-Eye, Cat's-Eye

Herbs/Plants - Acorns, Apples, Aster, Blackberry, Chamomile, Chrysanthemum, Corn, Fern, Gourds, Grain, Grapes, Hazel, Hops, Ivy, Marigold, Milkweed, Nuts, Pomegranate, Pumpkin, Rose, Rue, Saffron, Sage, Solomon's Seal, Sunflower, Thistle, Tobacco, Wheat, Yarrow

Symbols of Mabon - Cornucopia, Rattles, Sun Wheels

Gods - Archangel Michael, Bacchus, Cernunnos, Dagda, Dionysus, Dumuzi, Green Man, Mabon ap Modron, Thoth

Goddesses - Arawn, Ashtoreth, Ceridwen, Demeter & Persephone, Epona, Freya, Hathor, Inanna, Ishtar, Isis, Kore, Modrun, Morrigan, Venus

Wiccan Sabbats Rituals & Spells

Purpose:

Ingredients

When?

How?

Variations

Notes

My Altar and Sabbat Shrine

Sabbat Recipes

Samhain

October 31st.

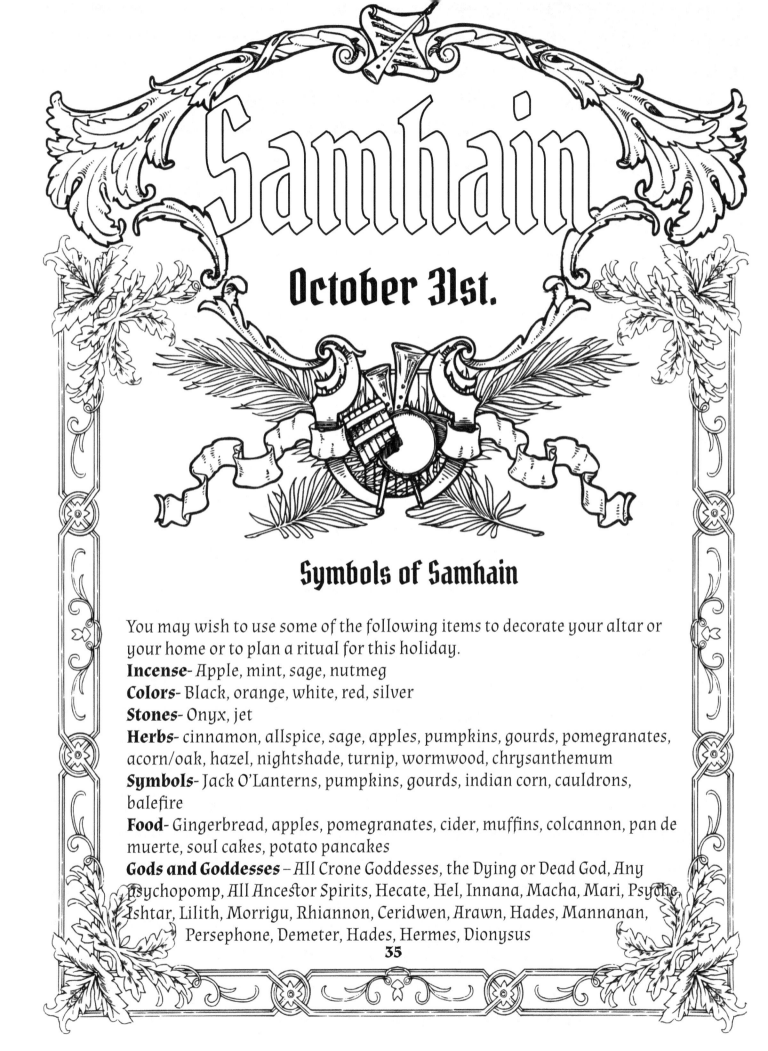

Symbols of Samhain

You may wish to use some of the following items to decorate your altar or your home or to plan a ritual for this holiday.

Incense- Apple, mint, sage, nutmeg

Colors- Black, orange, white, red, silver

Stones- Onyx, jet

Herbs- cinnamon, allspice, sage, apples, pumpkins, gourds, pomegranates, acorn/oak, hazel, nightshade, turnip, wormwood, chrysanthemum

Symbols- Jack O'Lanterns, pumpkins, gourds, indian corn, cauldrons, balefire

Food- Gingerbread, apples, pomegranates, cider, muffins, colcannon, pan de muerte, soul cakes, potato pancakes

Gods and Goddesses – All Crone Goddesses, the Dying or Dead God, Any psychopomp, All Ancestor Spirits, Hecate, Hel, Innana, Macha, Mari, Psyche, Ishtar, Lilith, Morrigu, Rhiannon, Ceridwen, Arawn, Hades, Mannanan, Persephone, Demeter, Hades, Hermes, Dionysus

Wiccan Sabbats Rituals & Spells

Purpose:

Ingredients

When?

How?

Variations

Notes

My Altar and Sabbat Shrine

Sabbat Recipes

Chapter 2

Wiccan Religion Gods & Goddesses

Notes for Chapter 2

Horned God

Creating a Devotional Practice

Ritual Planner

Organize your ritual planning with this one easy to use one page worksheet has space for all the information you need to plan, carry out, and look back at your rituals.

Intent Purpose _____

_____

_____

Date _____ Time _____

Astrological & Planetary Influences _____

Moon   Sun

Place _____ _____ _____

(significance) _____

Space set up_____

_____

Grounding Technique _____

Call Corners _____

Divine _____

Words of Power

_____

_____

_____

_____

Method to raise energy_____ Release _____

Offerings & Gratitude _____

_____

Open circle_____

Celebrate_____

Tools

_____

_____

_____

_____

_____

_____

_____

_____

Dress

_____

_____

_____

_____

_____

_____

_____

_____

_____

_____

After Ritual Thoughts

_____

_____

_____

_____

_____

_____

_____

_____

_____

_____

_____

Ritual Planner

Organize your ritual planning with this one easy to use one page worksheet has space for all the information you need to plan, carry out, and look back at your rituals.

Intent Purpose _____

_____

_____

Date _____ Time _____

Astrological & Planetary Influences _____

Moon   Sun

Place _____ _____

(significance) _____

Space set up_____

_____

Grounding Technique _____

Call Corners _____

Divine _____

Words of Power

_____

_____

_____

_____

_____

Method to raise energy_____ Release _____

Offerings & Gratitude _____

_____

Open circle_____

Celebrate_____

Tools

_____
_____
_____
_____
_____
_____
_____
_____

Dress

_____
_____
_____
_____
_____
_____
_____
_____
_____
_____

After Ritual Thoughts

_____
_____
_____
_____
_____
_____
_____
_____
_____

Reexamine & Evaluate the Final Purpose of the Spell

Signs of a Spell Working

My Feelings & Emotions

Coincidences:

Dreams:

New Opportunities:

Indirect Indicators:

Increased Contact:

Poseidon

Color it!
So mote it be!

Creating a Devotional Practice

Ritual Planner

Organize your ritual planning with this one easy to use one page worksheet has space for all the information you need to plan, carry out, and look back at your rituals.

Intent Purpose _____
_____
_____

Date _____ Time _____

Astrological & Planetary Influences _____

Moon   Sun

Place _____ _____ _____

(significance) _____

Space set up_____
_____

Grounding Technique _____

Call Corners _____

Divine _____

Words of Power

_____
_____
_____
_____
_____

Method to raise energy_____ Release _____

Offerings & Gratitude _____
_____

Open circle_____

Celebrate_____

Tools
_____
_____
_____
_____
_____
_____
_____
_____

Dress
_____
_____
_____
_____
_____
_____
_____
_____
_____
_____

After Ritual Thoughts
_____
_____
_____
_____
_____
_____
_____
_____
_____

Ritual Planner

Organize your ritual planning with this one easy to use one page worksheet has space for all the information you need to plan, carry out, and look back at your rituals.

Intent Purpose _____

_____

_____

Date _____ Time _____

Astrological & Planetary Influences _____

Moon   Sun

Place _____ _____ _____

(significance) _____

Space set up_____

_____

Grounding Technique _____

Call Corners _____

Divine _____

Words of Power

_____

_____

_____

_____

Method to raise energy_____ Release _____

Offerings & Gratitude _____

_____

Open circle_____

Celebrate_____

Tools

_____
_____
_____
_____
_____
_____
_____
_____
_____

Dress

_____
_____
_____
_____
_____
_____
_____

After Ritual Thoughts

_____
_____
_____
_____
_____
_____
_____
_____
_____
_____
_____

Reexamine & Evaluate the Final Purpose of the Spell

Signs of a Spell Working

My Feelings & Emotions

_____
_____
_____
_____
_____
_____
_____
_____

Coincidences:

_____
_____
_____
_____
_____
_____
_____

Dreams:

_____
_____
_____
_____
_____
_____
_____
_____

New Opportunities:

_____
_____
_____
_____
_____
_____
_____

Indirect Indicators:

_____
_____
_____
_____
_____
_____
_____

Increased Contact:

_____
_____
_____
_____
_____
_____

Aidoneus & Persephone

Color it!
So mote it be!

Creating a Devotional Practice

Ritual Planner

Organize your ritual planning with this one easy to use one page worksheet has space for all the information you need to plan, carry out, and look back at your rituals.

Intent Purpose _____

_____

_____

Date _____ Time _____

Astrological & Planetary Influences _____

Moon   Sun

Place _____ _____ _____

(significance) _____

Space set up _____

_____

Grounding Technique _____

Call Corners _____

Divine _____

Words of Power

_____

_____

_____

_____

_____

Method to raise energy_____ Release _____

Offerings & Gratitude _____

_____

Open circle_____

Celebrate_____

Tools

_____
_____
_____
_____
_____
_____
_____

Dress

_____
_____
_____
_____
_____
_____
_____
_____
_____

After Ritual Thoughts

_____
_____
_____
_____
_____
_____
_____
_____
_____

Ritual Planner

Organize your ritual planning with this one easy to use one page worksheet has space for all the information you need to plan, carry out, and look back at your rituals.

Intent Purpose _____

_____

_____

Date _____ Time _____

Astrological & Planetary Influences _____

Moon   Sun

Place _____ _____

(significance) _____

Space set up _____

_____

Grounding Technique _____

Call Corners _____

Divine _____

Words of Power

_____

_____

_____

_____

_____

Method to raise energy_____ Release _____

Offerings & Gratitude _____

_____

Open circle_____

Celebrate_____

Tools

_____
_____
_____
_____
_____
_____
_____
_____
_____

Dress

_____
_____
_____
_____
_____
_____
_____
_____
_____
_____

After Ritual Thoughts

_____
_____
_____
_____
_____
_____
_____
_____
_____

Reexamine & Evaluate the Final Purpose of the Spell

Signs of a Spell Working

My Feelings & Emotions

Coincidences:

Dreams:

New Opportunities:

Indirect Indicators:

Increased Contact:

Vulcan

Color it!
So mote it be!

59

Creating a Devotional Practice

Ritual Planner

Organize your ritual planning with this one easy to use one page worksheet has space for all the information you need to plan, carry out, and look back at your rituals.

Intent Purpose _____

_____

_____

Date _____ Time _____

Astrological & Planetary Influences _____

Moon   Sun

Place _____ _____

(significance) _____

Space set up _____

_____

Grounding Technique _____

Call Corners _____

Divine _____

Words of Power

_____

_____

_____

_____

Method to raise energy_____ Release _____

Offerings & Gratitude _____

Open circle_____

Celebrate_____

Tools

_____
_____
_____
_____
_____
_____
_____
_____

Dress

_____
_____
_____
_____
_____
_____
_____
_____
_____
_____

After Ritual Thoughts

_____
_____
_____
_____
_____
_____
_____
_____
_____

Ritual Planner

Organize your ritual planning with this one easy to use one page
worksheet has space for all the information you need to plan,
carry out, and look back at your rituals.

Intent Purpose _____

_____

_____

Date _____ Time _____

Astrological & Planetary Influences _____

Moon

Sun

Place _____ _____ _____

(significance) _____

Space set up_____

_____

Grounding Technique _____

Call Corners _____

Divine _____

Words of Power

_____

_____

_____

_____

Method to raise energy_____ Release _____

Offerings & Gratitude _____

_____

Open circle_____

Celebrate_____

Tools

_____

Dress

_____

**After Ritual
Thoughts**

_____

62

Reexamine & Evaluate the Final Purpose of the Spell

Signs of a Spell Working

My Feelings & Emotions

_____
_____
_____
_____
_____
_____
_____
_____

Coincidences:

_____
_____
_____
_____
_____
_____
_____
_____

Dreams:

_____
_____
_____
_____
_____
_____
_____

New Opportunities:

_____
_____
_____
_____
_____
_____
_____

Indirect Indicators:

_____
_____
_____
_____
_____
_____
_____

Increased Contact:

_____
_____
_____
_____
_____
_____
_____

Ceres

Color it!
So mote it be!

Creating a Devotional Practice

Ritual Planner

Organize your ritual planning with this one easy to use one page worksheet has space for all the information you need to plan, carry out, and look back at your rituals.

Intent Purpose _____

_____

_____

Date _____ Time _____

Astrological & Planetary Influences _____

Moon   Sun

Place _____ _____ _____

(significance) _____

Space set up_____

_____

Grounding Technique _____

Call Corners _____

Divine _____

Words of Power

_____
_____
_____
_____
_____

Method to raise energy_____ Release _____

Offerings & Gratitude _____

_____

Open circle_____

Celebrate_____

Tools

_____
_____
_____
_____
_____
_____
_____
_____
_____

Dress

_____
_____
_____
_____
_____
_____
_____
_____
_____
_____

After Ritual Thoughts

_____
_____
_____
_____
_____
_____
_____
_____
_____
_____

Ritual Planner

Organize your ritual planning with this one easy to use one page worksheet has space for all the information you need to plan, carry out, and look back at your rituals.

Intent Purpose _____

_____

_____

Date _____ Time _____

Astrological & Planetary Influences _____

Moon   Sun

Place _____ _____ _____

(significance) _____

Space set up _____

_____

Grounding Technique _____

Call Corners _____

Divine _____

Words of Power

_____

_____

_____

_____

Method to raise energy_____ Release _____

Offerings & Gratitude _____

_____

Open circle_____

Celebrate_____

Tools

_____

_____

Dress

_____

_____

After Ritual Thoughts

_____

_____

Reexamine & Evaluate the Final Purpose of the Spell

Signs of a Spell Working

My Feelings & Emotions

Coincidences:

Dreams:

New Opportunities:

Indirect Indicators:

Increased Contact:

The God

Creating a Devotional Practice

Ritual Planner

Organize your ritual planning with this one easy to use one page worksheet has space for all the information you need to plan, carry out, and look back at your rituals.

Intent Purpose _____

_____

_____

Date _____ Time _____

Astrological & Planetary Influences _____

Moon   Sun

Place _____

(significance) _____

Space set up_____

_____

Grounding Technique _____

Call Corners _____

Divine _____

Words of Power

_____

_____

_____

_____

Method to raise energy_____ Release _____

Offerings & Gratitude _____

Open circle_____

Celebrate_____

Tools

_____
_____
_____
_____
_____
_____
_____

Dress

_____
_____
_____
_____
_____
_____
_____
_____

After Ritual Thoughts

_____
_____
_____
_____
_____
_____
_____
_____

Ritual Planner

Organize your ritual planning with this one easy to use one page worksheet has space for all the information you need to plan, carry out, and look back at your rituals.

Intent Purpose _____

_____

_____

Date _____ Time _____

Astrological & Planetary Influences _____

Moon   Sun

Place _____ _____ _____

(significance) _____

Space set up_____

_____

Grounding Technique _____

Call Corners _____

Divine _____

Words of Power

_____
_____
_____
_____
_____

Method to raise energy_____ Release _____

Offerings & Gratitude _____

_____

Open circle_____

Celebrate_____

Tools

_____
_____
_____
_____
_____
_____
_____
_____

Dress

_____
_____
_____
_____
_____
_____
_____
_____

After Ritual Thoughts

_____
_____
_____
_____
_____
_____
_____

74

Reexamine & Evaluate the Final Purpose of the Spell

Signs of a Spell Working

My Feelings & Emotions

Coincidences:

Dreams:

New Opportunities:

Indirect Indicators:

Increased Contact:

Aphrodite

Color it!
So mote it be!

Creating a Devotional Practice

Ritual Planner

Organize your ritual planning with this one easy to use one page worksheet has space for all the information you need to plan, carry out, and look back at your rituals.

Intent Purpose _____

_____

_____

Date _____   Time _____

Astrological & Planetary Influences _____

Moon   Sun

Place _____   _____

(significance) _____

Space set up_____

_____

Grounding Technique _____

Call Corners _____

Divine _____

Words of Power

_____

_____

_____

_____

_____

Method to raise energy_____ Release _____

Offerings & Gratitude _____

_____

Open circle_____

Celebrate_____

Tools

_____

_____

_____

_____

_____

_____

_____

_____

_____

Dress

_____

_____

_____

_____

_____

_____

_____

_____

After Ritual Thoughts

_____

_____

_____

_____

_____

_____

_____

_____

_____

_____

Ritual Planner

Organize your ritual planning with this one easy to use one page worksheet has space for all the information you need to plan, carry out, and look back at your rituals.

Intent Purpose _____

_____

_____

Date _____ Time _____

Astrological & Planetary Influences _____

Moon   Sun

Place _____ _____ _____

(significance) _____

Space set up_____

_____

Grounding Technique _____

Call Corners _____

Divine _____

Words of Power

_____
_____
_____
_____
_____

Method to raise energy_____ Release _____

Offerings & Gratitude _____

_____

Open circle_____

Celebrate_____

Tools

_____
_____
_____
_____
_____
_____
_____
_____
_____

Dress

_____
_____
_____
_____
_____
_____
_____
_____
_____

After Ritual Thoughts

_____
_____
_____
_____
_____
_____
_____
_____

Reexamine & Evaluate the Final Purpose of the Spell

Signs of a Spell Working

My Feelings & Emotions

Coincidences:

Dreams:

New Opportunities:

Indirect Indicators:

Increased Contact:

Ares

Creating a Devotional Practice

Ritual Planner

Organize your ritual planning with this one easy to use one page worksheet has space for all the information you need to plan, carry out, and look back at your rituals.

Intent Purpose _____

_____

_____

Date _____ Time _____

Astrological & Planetary Influences _____

Moon   Sun

Place _____ _____ _____

(significance) _____

Space set up_____

_____

Grounding Technique _____

Call Corners _____

Divine _____

Words of Power

_____

_____

_____

_____

_____

Method to raise energy_____ Release _____

Offerings & Gratitude _____

_____

Open circle_____

Celebrate_____

Tools

_____
_____
_____
_____
_____
_____
_____
_____

Dress

_____
_____
_____
_____
_____
_____
_____
_____
_____
_____
_____
_____

After Ritual Thoughts

_____
_____
_____
_____
_____
_____
_____
_____
_____
_____

Ritual Planner

Organize your ritual planning with this one easy to use one page worksheet has space for all the information you need to plan, carry out, and look back at your rituals.

Intent Purpose _____

_____

_____

Date _____ Time _____

Astrological & Planetary Influences _____

Moon   Sun

Place _____ _____ _____

(significance) _____

Space set up_____

_____

Grounding Technique _____

Call Corners _____

Divine _____

Words of Power

_____

_____

_____

_____

Method to raise energy_____ Release _____

Offerings & Gratitude _____

_____

Open circle_____

Celebrate_____

Tools

_____

_____

_____

_____

_____

_____

_____

_____

_____

_____

_____

_____

Dress

_____

_____

_____

_____

_____

_____

_____

_____

_____

_____

After Ritual Thoughts

_____

_____

_____

_____

_____

_____

_____

_____

_____

_____

Reexamine & Evaluate the Final Purpose of the Spell

Signs of a Spell Working

My Feelings & Emotions

Coincidences:

Dreams:

New Opportunities:

Indirect Indicators:

Increased Contact:

Zeus

Creating a Devotional Practice

Ritual Planner

Organize your ritual planning with this one easy to use one page worksheet has space for all the information you need to plan, carry out, and look back at your rituals.

Intent Purpose _____

_____

_____

Date _____ Time _____

Astrological & Planetary Influences _____

Moon   Sun

Place _____ _____ _____

(significance) _____

Space set up_____

_____

Grounding Technique _____

Call Corners _____

Divine _____

Words of Power

_____

_____

_____

_____

_____

Method to raise energy_____ Release _____

Offerings & Gratitude _____

_____

Open circle_____

Celebrate_____

Tools

_____
_____
_____
_____
_____
_____
_____
_____
_____

Dress

_____
_____
_____
_____
_____
_____
_____
_____
_____
_____
_____

After Ritual Thoughts

_____
_____
_____
_____
_____
_____
_____
_____
_____

Ritual Planner

Organize your ritual planning with this one easy to use one page worksheet has space for all the information you need to plan, carry out, and look back at your rituals.

Intent Purpose _____

_____

_____

Date _____ Time _____

Astrological & Planetary Influences _____

Moon   Sun

Place _____ _____ _____

(significance) _____

Space set up _____

_____

Grounding Technique _____

Call Corners _____

Divine _____

Words of Power

_____

_____

_____

_____

_____

Method to raise energy_____ Release _____

Offerings & Gratitude _____

_____

Open circle_____

Celebrate_____

Tools
_____
_____
_____
_____
_____
_____
_____
_____

Dress
_____
_____
_____
_____
_____
_____
_____
_____

After Ritual Thoughts
_____
_____
_____
_____
_____
_____
_____
_____

Reexamine & Evaluate the Final Purpose of the Spell

Signs of a Spell Working

My Feelings & Emotions

Coincidences:

Dreams:

New Opportunities:

Indirect Indicators:

Increased Contact:

Rhea & Cronus

Color it!
So mote it be!

Creating a Devotional Practice

Ritual Planner

Organize your ritual planning with this one easy to use one page worksheet has space for all the information you need to plan, carry out, and look back at your rituals.

Intent Purpose _____

_____

_____

Date _____ Time _____

Astrological & Planetary Influences _____

Moon   Sun

Place _____ _____ _____

(significance) _____

Space set up_____

_____

Grounding Technique _____

Call Corners _____

Divine _____

Words of Power

_____

_____

_____

_____

_____

Method to raise energy_____ Release _____

Offerings & Gratitude _____

_____

Open circle_____

Celebrate_____

Tools

_____
_____
_____
_____
_____
_____
_____
_____
_____
_____
_____

Dress

_____
_____
_____
_____
_____
_____
_____
_____
_____
_____
_____
_____
_____
_____

After Ritual Thoughts

_____
_____
_____
_____
_____
_____
_____
_____
_____

Ritual Planner

Organize your ritual planning with this one easy to use one page worksheet has space for all the information you need to plan, carry out, and look back at your rituals.

Intent Purpose _____

_____

_____

Date _____ Time _____

Astrological & Planetary Influences _____

Moon   Sun

Place _____ _____ _____

(significance) _____

Space set up _____

_____

Grounding Technique _____

Call Corners _____

Divine _____

Words of Power

_____

_____

_____

_____

_____

Method to raise energy_____ Release _____

Offerings & Gratitude _____

_____

Open circle_____

Celebrate_____

Tools

_____
_____
_____
_____
_____
_____
_____
_____
_____
_____

Dress

_____
_____
_____
_____
_____
_____
_____
_____
_____

After Ritual Thoughts

_____
_____
_____
_____
_____
_____
_____
_____
_____

Reexamine & Evaluate the Final Purpose of the Spell

Signs of a Spell Working

My Feelings & Emotions

Coincidences:

Dreams:

New Opportunities:

Indirect Indicators:

Increased Contact:

Chapter 3

Magic Healing Herbs for Rituals

Notes for Chapter 3

Agrimony

Agrimony is excellent for the digestive system, cuts, bruises, and throat problems. It is also useful for psychic protection, as it successfully returns negative energies to the sender and helps for a peaceful sleep.

Agrimony could be used in guarding sachets and as part of a sleep pillow for times when you are exhausted and experience difficulty in rest. Ruled by Jupiter

Allspice

Allspice is used for healing for all aspects of life. Excellent for digestive organs, rheumatism, and neuralgia. We frequently burn it as incense to promote good luck and to attract money.
Ruled by Mars

Aloe Vera

Aloe Vera soothes burns and wounds, and it is useful in treating a lack of appetite, bowel, and menstrual problems. It is famous as a protective plant and brings luck and prosperity to the house.
Ruled by the Moon

Angelica

Angelica is known to relieve the plague during the Middle Ages. It is a natural energizer and is suitable for respiratory and liver problems and for improving blood circulation.

It is protective, especially for children, when worn as an amulet. You can grow it in the garden to protect your garden and home. People also believe that this plant will give you a long life and strength against illness. Ruled by the Sun

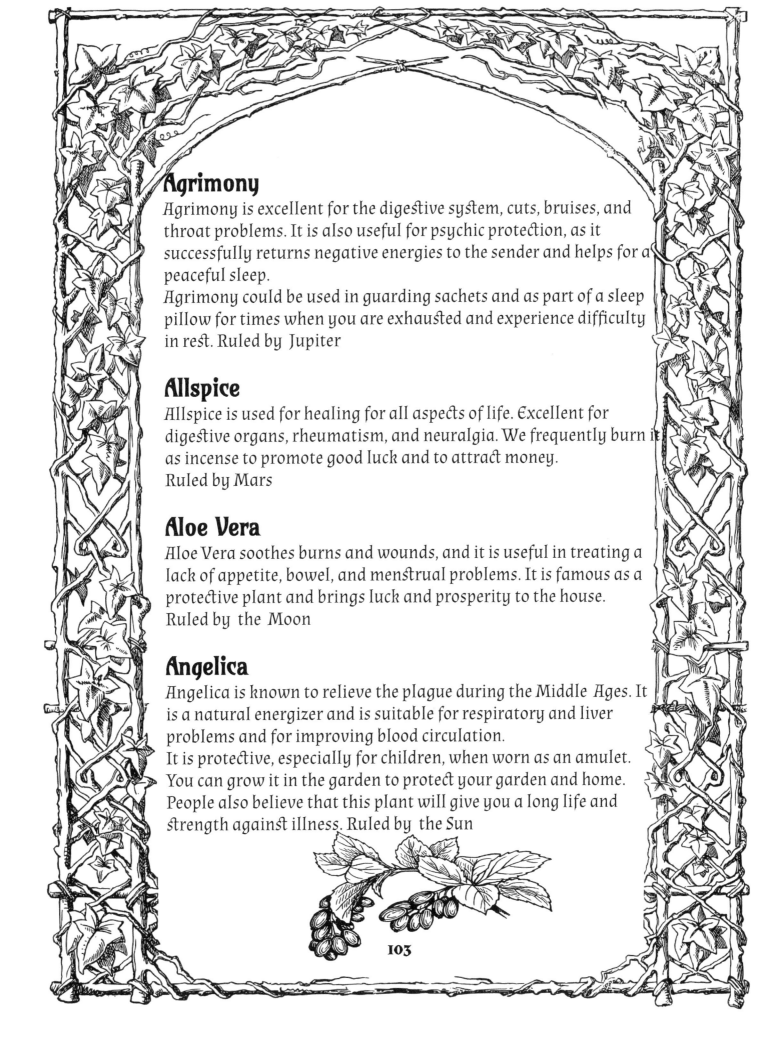

How to Use Herbs in my Magical Workings?

Anise (aniseed)

Anise calms the nervous system and relieves coughs and lung problems. It is a very soothing herb, excellent for skin problems. It guards against all negative influences, especially in the home, including external hostility and bad dreams. A sachet close to the bed keeps you young. Ruled by Jupiter

Apple

Apple is good for fevers and vomiting. It has excellent revitalizing power and fertility. It is primarily used for healing babies and youngsters. It will also restore youthful optimism, improve relationships, and affect the increase of hope. It enhances inner beauty and boosts self-esteem, especially if a person is worried or being harassed.

Apple will enhance all forms of new growth and will restore fertility to gardens and areas of land that have been made barren or urbanized. Ruled by Venus

Ash

For Celts, Ash was a sacred tree. During the late nineteenth century in Killura, Ireland, it was used as a charm against drowning. It was often used to cure a toothache, rickets, hernias, or wounds that would not heal.

The leaves and powdered bark are very efficient for all healing and for endowing good lasting health. It is also useful for protection at sea while sailing or swimming. Ruled by the Sun

How to Use Herbs in my Magical Workings?

Aspen

The Aspen is known as the shiver-tree because the leaves shook even when there was no breeze. By sympathetic magic, it was believed that 'like cures like,' and so the Aspen was said to have the power to cure fevers and diseases involving trembling or extremities from cold. It is known to be beneficial for eloquence.

It is a protective herb and can be used in anti-theft and robbery sachets hidden in your home or your car.

Ruled by Saturn, in his most favorable appearances

Basil

Basil clears the mind and reduces stress. It can be used for stomach disorders and menstruation problems, including ulcers. It also removes toxins, so it is suitable for anti-pollution rituals. Basil also repels harmful insects and restores peaceful sleep.

It is an herb of love and faithfulness and also attracts abundance and accomplishment. As a protective herb, it is suitable for overcoming the fear of flying. Ruled by Mars

Bay

Bay can be applied for most digestive disorders, for stress, and psychosomatic illness. It offers psychic protection and will heal grief. It purifies all forms of pollution and negativity, provides strength and endurance, and encourages devotion. Ruled by the Sun

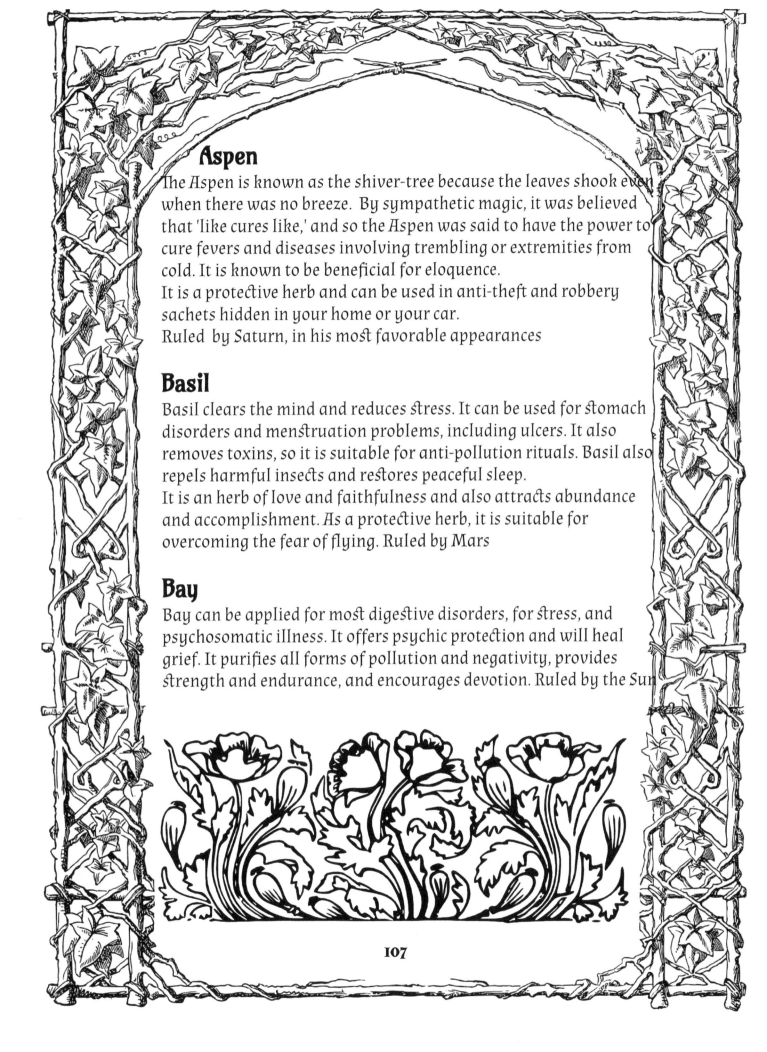

How to Use Herbs in my Magical Workings?

Bistort

Bistort is potent in relieving injuries of all kinds, emotional as well as physical, mouth, throat, and tongue problems, mainly when mixed with echinacea, myrrh, and goldenseal. It helps fertility, so it can be carried out by women who hope to become pregnant.

It repels those who come to your home with malice or ill-intention. Bistort also increases abundance and prosperity and psychic awareness. Ruled by Saturn

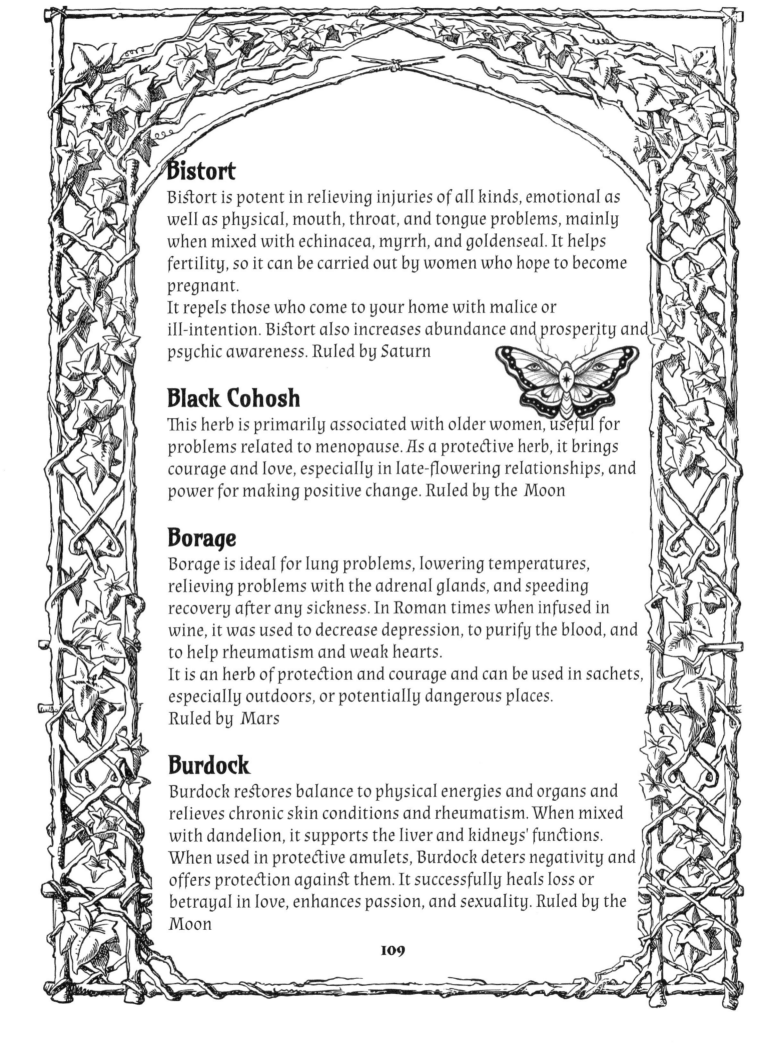

Black Cohosh

This herb is primarily associated with older women, useful for problems related to menopause. As a protective herb, it brings courage and love, especially in late-flowering relationships, and power for making positive change. Ruled by the Moon

Borage

Borage is ideal for lung problems, lowering temperatures, relieving problems with the adrenal glands, and speeding recovery after any sickness. In Roman times when infused in wine, it was used to decrease depression, to purify the blood, and to help rheumatism and weak hearts.

It is an herb of protection and courage and can be used in sachets, especially outdoors, or potentially dangerous places.
Ruled by Mars

Burdock

Burdock restores balance to physical energies and organs and relieves chronic skin conditions and rheumatism. When mixed with dandelion, it supports the liver and kidneys' functions. When used in protective amulets, Burdock deters negativity and offers protection against them. It successfully heals loss or betrayal in love, enhances passion, and sexuality. Ruled by the Moon

How to Use Herbs in my Magical Workings?

Caraway

Caraway relieves menstrual problems and nourishes nursing mothers. It is useful for all digestive disorders, coughs, bruises, and helps to improve memory. It is protective against all sources of negativity, especially against theft and vandalism. It is also an aphrodisiac that can inspire or arouse passion. Ruled by Mercury

Catnip

Catnip will help influenza, prolonged fevers, viruses, and respiratory problems, mainly when mixed with elder and yarrow in sachets or poppets. It is beneficial for children and cats. When mixed with rose petals, it makes a great love sachet. Catnip attracts good fortune and benign forces when growing around the home. It also enhances the inner beauty and domestic joy. Ruled by Venus

Chamomile

Chamomile is the most gentle and soothing herbs. It has many uses, as relieving insomnia, soothing anxiety, and calming hyperactive children. It is wonderful for all digestive problems, especially in babies. No baby's room should be without its Lavender, Chamomile and Fennel sachet as a gift for a newborn. Chamomile relieves eye problems in children and adults.

It is used in charms to attract abundance and prosperity. It is suitable for attracting new love, meditation, family happiness, and the growth of trust after betrayal and loss. It is protective and stops those who would harm you. Ruled by the Sun

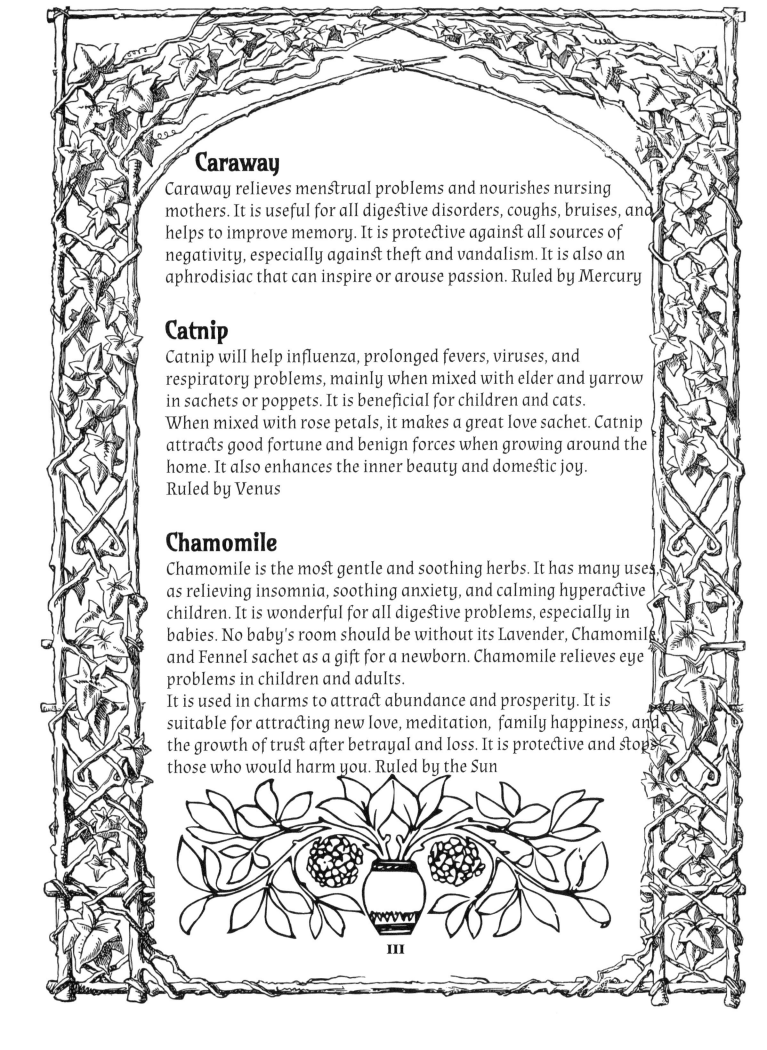

How to Use Herbs in my Magical Workings?

Cloves

Cloves are excellent for reducing tooth pains, nausea in pregnancy, blood circulation problems, back, and lung problems. As part of an amulet or sachet, cloves will prevent gossip, hatred, and resentment against the wearer and encourage the user to learn new skills. Cloves are a natural aphrodisiac that both attracts love and stimulates sexual feelings. For those who have suffered loss, cloves offer comfort. Ruled by Jupiter

Coltsfoot

Coltsfoot is possibly the best herbal solution for respiratory problems, particularly persistent dry coughs, bronchitis, asthma, and emphysema. It also soothes the stomach and fights fluid retention. It is traditionally used to induce peace of mind and in love rituals and sachets.
Coltsfoot also offers protection to horses and people who travel. Ruled by Venus

Comfrey

Comfrey soothes burns, cuts, asthma, and coughs and speeds the healing process. Comfrey offers protection for people while traveling and, if placed in
a suitcase, will guard your belongings against loss or theft. It is a true bringer of luck and money. If a person has suffered financial or material loss, it can be added to abundance sachets.
Ruled by Saturn

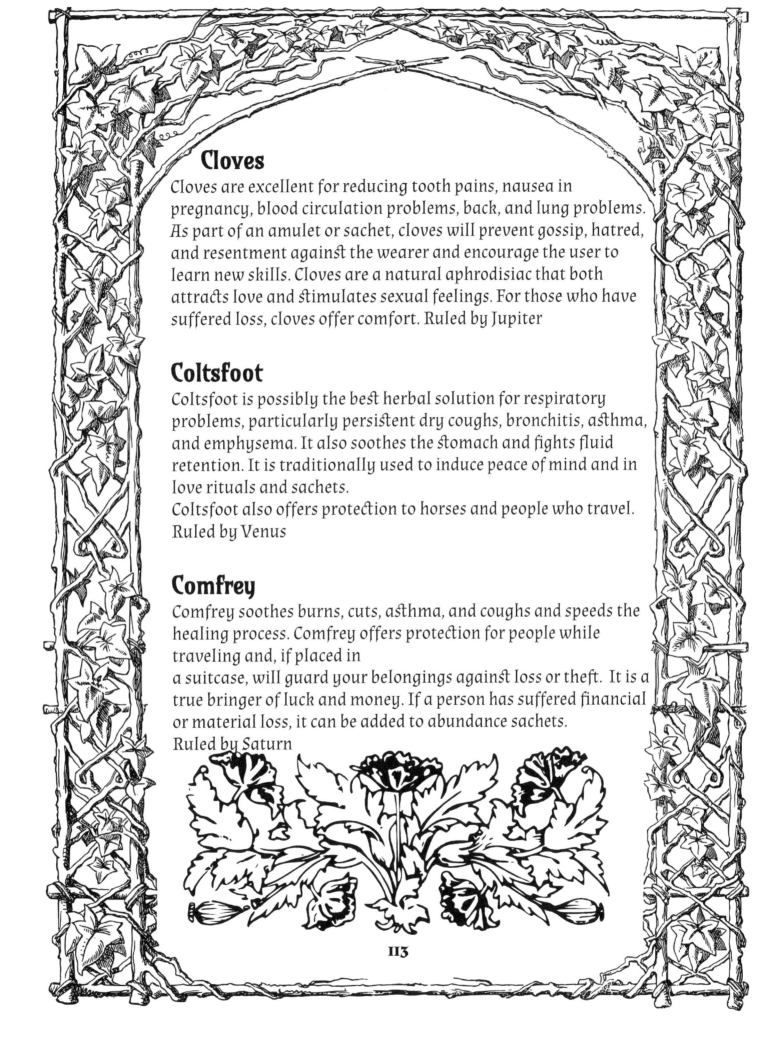

How to Use Herbs in my Magical Workings?

Dandelion

Dandelion helps to remove obstructions and is suitable for the gallbladder, liver, spleen, and kidneys. It detoxifies the system, relieves fluid retention, premenstrual tension, and encourages blood circulation.

It promotes psychic awareness, carrying feelings between lovers. It is commonly used in the country love divination to answer questions concerning a partner's fidelity and intentions.
Ruled by Jupiter

Dill

Dill is an herb for infants and nursing mothers' well-being, assisting lactation, and bringing ease and quiet sleep when baby cries or fusses frequently.

It is an herb of love and passion and can also be used in love and protection sachets, especially for the homes. It will repel intruders and malice, so place it in a sachet near entrances. Add it to your nursery sachets. Ruled by Mercury

Echinacea (purple cornflower)

Echinacea is a natural antibiotic that triggers your immune system. It increases the production of white blood cells, aids the efficient functioning of the lymph glands. Excellent for building up immunity to a person who has been ill or is physically vulnerable. Heals mouth sores, gums, or wounds.

Echinacea is an herb of awareness and spiritual growth. It is used where altruism and idealism are to the fore, promotes spiritual dreams. Ruled by Jupiter

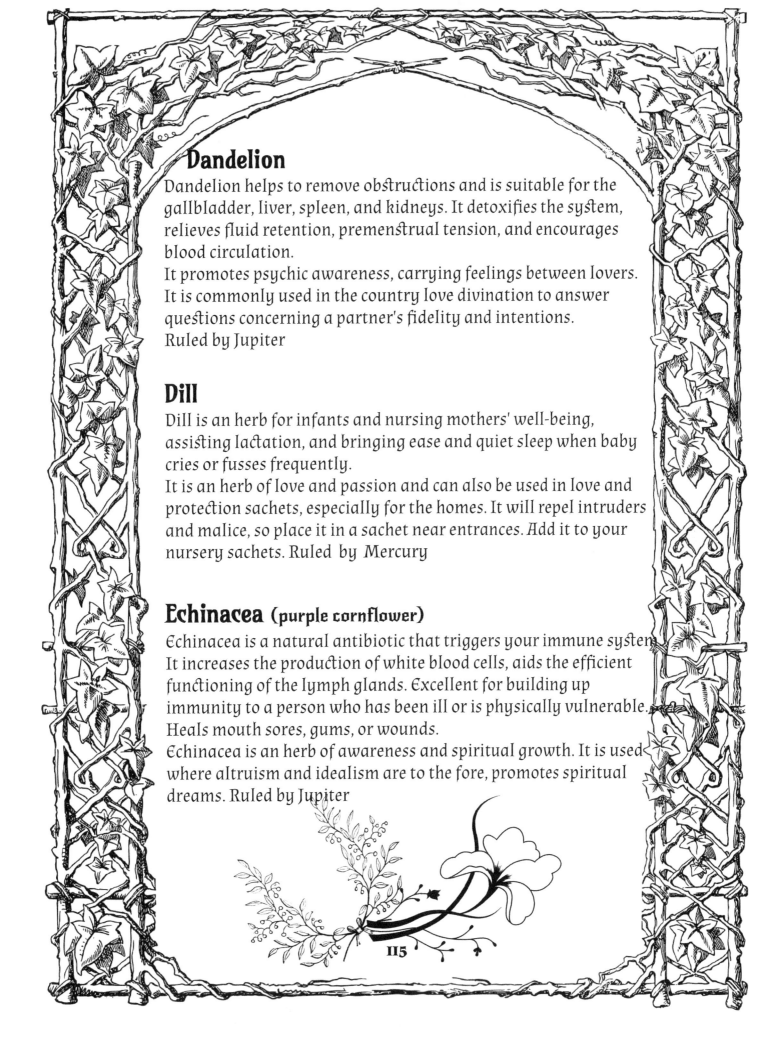

How to Use Herbs in my Magical Workings?

Elder

Elder is favorite to the Romany gypsies as a base for various remedies. It is a powerful antiseptic and can be used to treat sprains, wounds, rheumatism, influenza, respiratory complaints, hay fever, and sinusitis. It brings peaceful sleep, presenting insomnia.
Elder offers protection from hatred to you, and your home from storm destruction and other weather extremes. It brings health, wealth, and happiness, especially a marital joy to a new bride or groom. Ruled by Venus

Elecampane (elfwort)

Elecampane is useful for all respiratory complaints, coughs, especially in children; it helps asthma, bronchitis asthma, loss of appetite, and general failure to thrive.
As its name suggests, it is associated with elves and faeries and is a natural love charm, potent in love sachets, amulets, and rituals for attraction. It is protective against all forms of hostility and increases psychic awareness. Ruled by Venus

Fennel

From Roman times, fennel has been famous for its effects on courage, stamina, and renewed strength and energy. It is useful for improving a sluggish metabolic rate, for reducing all swelling, especially fluid retention, premenstrual tension, aiding breastfeeding, and easing an infant's colic and restlessness. It cures sore eyes and coughs and improves mental alertness.
Fennel brings shield from unwanted visitors and all forms of external hostility. Ruled by Mercury

How to Use Herbs in my Magical Workings?

Ginger

Such appreciated in the East, ginger is used now in China to aid potency and ensure a long life. It warms the body, removing pain, particularly rheumatism, boosts the immune system, strengthens and heals the respiratory system.

It is useful for throat complaints, all sickness, and nausea, particularly during pregnancy and while traveling. Ginger should be added to your travel sachets.

Ginger is also often carried powdered in a little scent-bag in a pocket or purse to attract money, success, and love. It acts as a physical and emotional energizer. Ruled by Mars

Holy Thistle

Holy thistle is active in treating all liver, gallbladder, and spleen problems, help organs damaged by alcohol or hepatitis. It counters appetite loss and eases menopausal symptoms.

It is essentially a protective herb, used to keep away all negativity. It is an assistant to any spiritual work or contact with the higher self, angels, or spirit guides. It encourages altruism. Ruled by Mars

Hops

A gentle, safe, and powerful sedative, hops are used in treating insomnia, internal spasms triggered by stress and nervous tension. Hops will calm the entire nervous system and so can be used to treat coughs, bladder, and liver worsened by anxiety, bowel disorders with an agitation component, as skin problems with an emotional cause, and irritable bowel syndrome.

As a protective herb, hops will drive off dark thoughts, insecurities, and fears. Ruled by the Sun

How to Use Herbs in my Magical Workings?

Hyssop

For its capability to cleanse the body of illness, Hyssop is mentioned many times in the Bible. It soothes coughs, bronchitis, sore throats and viruses, tension and stress-related conditions, burns, ear pains, and problems, particularly in children.

It is essentially an herb of purifying and will help to banish sad thoughts, despair, and doubts, and leave a positive approach. Hyssop eliminates negativity from your home and from objects that have unwelcoming or depressed vibrations. Ruled by Jupiter

Juniper

Juniper is a natural antiseptic. It relieves gastrointestinal and digestive infections, rheumatism, arthritis, inflammation, joint and muscle pain. It also enhances male potency.

Juniper naturally purifies the home from past negative forces and future misfortune, especially at New Year. It also acts as an amulet against accidents, theft, and illness. Ruled by the Sun

Knotweed

Knotweed is a natural antiseptic that helps to heal contaminated wounds. It will prevent anxiety from evolving and calm nerves. It relieves muscle problems and is suitable for general health and improvement of conditions that induce immobility.

Knotweed increases passionate devotion and encourages fidelity, can be used to ensure that promises are kept, and for all rituals involving knots. Ruled by the Moon

How to Use Herbs in my Magical Workings?

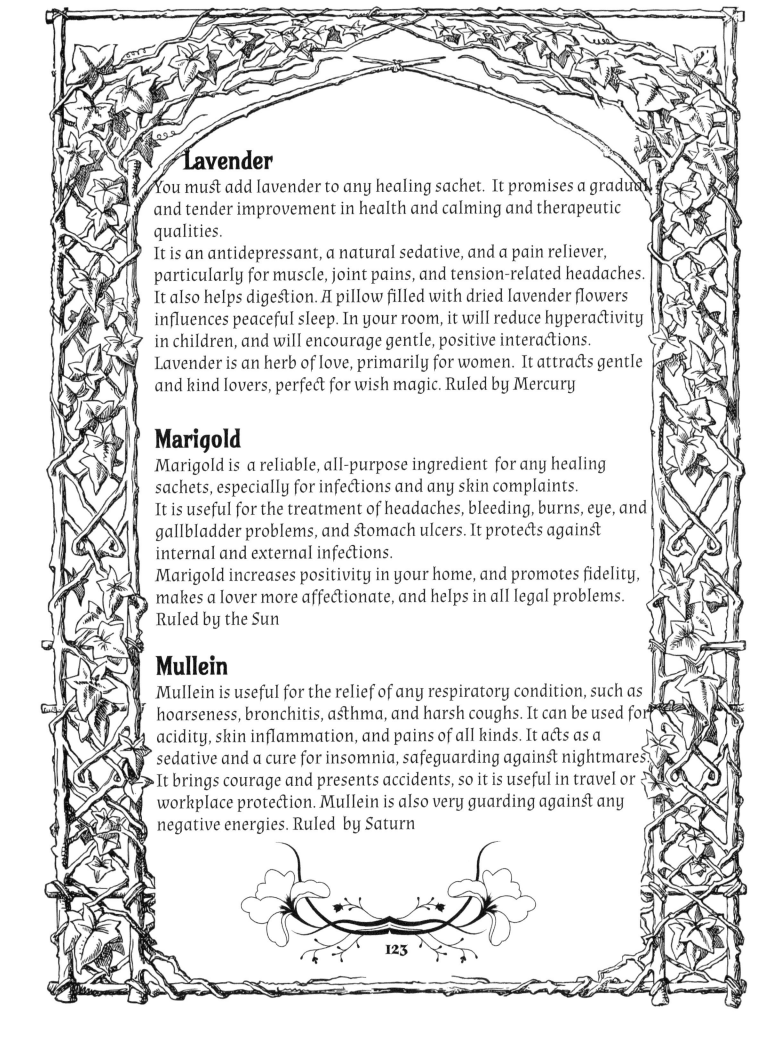

Lavender

You must add lavender to any healing sachet. It promises a gradual and tender improvement in health and calming and therapeutic qualities.

It is an antidepressant, a natural sedative, and a pain reliever, particularly for muscle, joint pains, and tension-related headaches. It also helps digestion. A pillow filled with dried lavender flowers influences peaceful sleep. In your room, it will reduce hyperactivity in children, and will encourage gentle, positive interactions.

Lavender is an herb of love, primarily for women. It attracts gentle and kind lovers, perfect for wish magic. Ruled by Mercury

Marigold

Marigold is a reliable, all-purpose ingredient for any healing sachets, especially for infections and any skin complaints.

It is useful for the treatment of headaches, bleeding, burns, eye, and gallbladder problems, and stomach ulcers. It protects against internal and external infections.

Marigold increases positivity in your home, and promotes fidelity, makes a lover more affectionate, and helps in all legal problems. Ruled by the Sun

Mullein

Mullein is useful for the relief of any respiratory condition, such as hoarseness, bronchitis, asthma, and harsh coughs. It can be used for acidity, skin inflammation, and pains of all kinds. It acts as a sedative and a cure for insomnia, safeguarding against nightmares. It brings courage and presents accidents, so it is useful in travel or workplace protection. Mullein is also very guarding against any negative energies. Ruled by Saturn

How to Use Herbs in my Magical Workings?

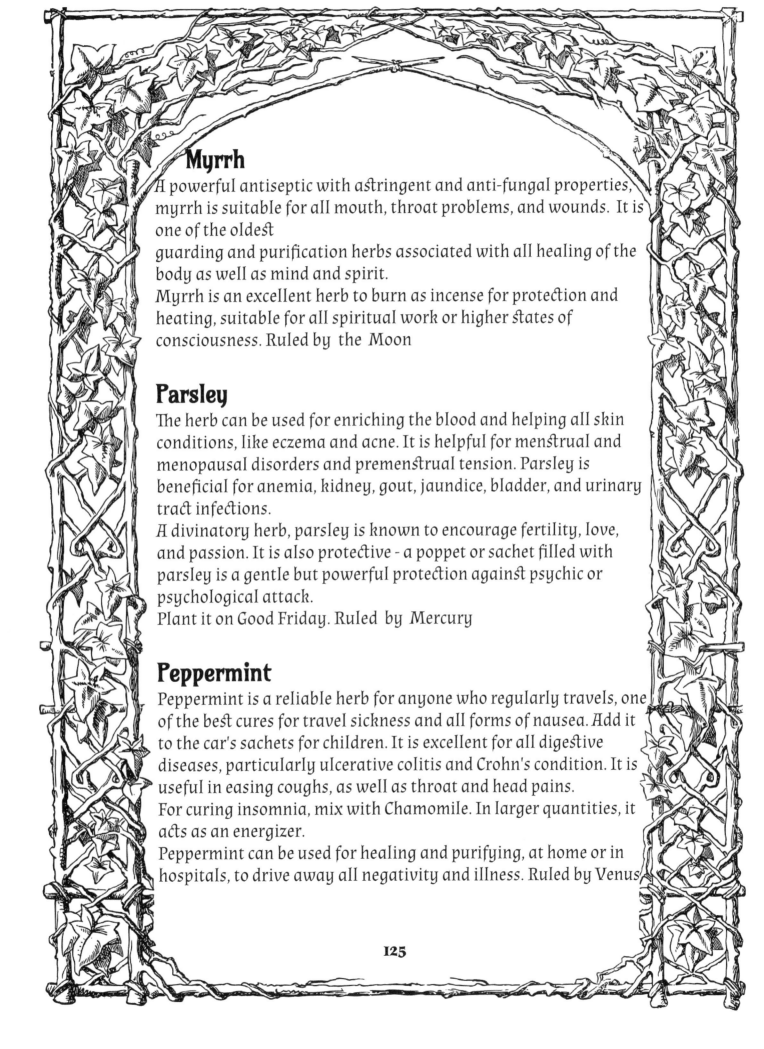

Myrrh

A powerful antiseptic with astringent and anti-fungal properties, myrrh is suitable for all mouth, throat problems, and wounds. It is one of the oldest

guarding and purification herbs associated with all healing of the body as well as mind and spirit.

Myrrh is an excellent herb to burn as incense for protection and heating, suitable for all spiritual work or higher states of consciousness. Ruled by the Moon

Parsley

The herb can be used for enriching the blood and helping all skin conditions, like eczema and acne. It is helpful for menstrual and menopausal disorders and premenstrual tension. Parsley is beneficial for anemia, kidney, gout, jaundice, bladder, and urinary tract infections.

A divinatory herb, parsley is known to encourage fertility, love, and passion. It is also protective - a poppet or sachet filled with parsley is a gentle but powerful protection against psychic or psychological attack.

Plant it on Good Friday. Ruled by Mercury

Peppermint

Peppermint is a reliable herb for anyone who regularly travels, one of the best cures for travel sickness and all forms of nausea. Add it to the car's sachets for children. It is excellent for all digestive diseases, particularly ulcerative colitis and Crohn's condition. It is useful in easing coughs, as well as throat and head pains.

For curing insomnia, mix with Chamomile. In larger quantities, it acts as an energizer.

Peppermint can be used for healing and purifying, at home or in hospitals, to drive away all negativity and illness. Ruled by Venus

How to Use Herbs in my Magical Workings?

Rose

An essential ingredient in healing sachets rose is potent in fighting infections and viruses of all kinds. It is excellent for relieving physical and emotional fatigue, hyperactivity, skin problems, and menstrual disorders.

Use rose in any love rituals to attract love and to give meaningful and prophetic dreams. Rose is also a symbol of bravery, especially the blood-red rose. Ruled by Venus

Rosemary

Rosemary reduces sciatica, muscular pain, headaches, depression, liver, and gallbladder problems. It assists digestion, improves blood circulation, and memory, helps with hair and scalp disorders, sharpens thoughts, and boosts energy levels.

Put a small amount of chopped rosemary in a muslin bag and add it to a bath. Rosemary is an old prescription for energy and purity of thoughts. As an herb of protection, rosemary drives away bad dreams. Use it in love sachets to attract lovers and heal negative or confrontational relationships.

Rosemary is also an herb of remembrance, especially of love, and can bring about reconciliation. Ruled by the Sun

St John's Wort (Hypericum)

Hypericum reduces depression, neuralgia, anxiety, headaches, and irritation during menopause. It is perfect for pain relief, fibrositis, rheumatism, and sciatica.

It is used as an anti-inflammatory and speeds the healing of burns and wounds. St John's Wort is the golden herb of summer, a symbol of the longest day of the year.

It offers potency and powers to attract love, mainly if picked at midnight on 23 June (the Eve of St John). During the century, Hypericum was worn in the battles for courage, or to bring decisiveness. Use it for protection, especially if combined with dill and vervain. Ruled by the Sun

How to Use Herbs in my Magical Workings?

Sage

Sage is a traditional culinary herb with many medical purposes and healing capabilities. In medieval times it was said:" Why should a man who has sage in his garden ever die?" Sage was called 'the holy herb' by the Romans and was extensively used by the Ancient Egyptians to cure male infertility.

Nowadays, the Chinese use sage to stimulate Yang as well as Yin energies.

Sage is very useful for prolonging life and health, strengthening the lungs, boosting the immune system, speeding recovery in instances of debilitating or chronic diseases, and helping to build up resistance to illness.

Sage relieves mental exhaustion and improves the ability to concentrate, so it is ideal in sachets mixed with rosemary for people under stress from tests or at work. It lifts depression and soothes anxieties.

Sage increases psychic awareness and allows flashes of past and future; it attracts good health, money, and gives protection for the home and family. Ruled by Jupiter

Tarragon

Tarragon is a mild stimulant, helps to overcome nervous exhaustion that can prevent your relaxation, soothing anxieties, so sleep comes quickly.

It is also useful for stimulating the kidneys and is a traditional remedy for toothache and digestive problems.

Throughout the centuries, it was associated with dragons and serpent goddesses and the ability to cure snake bites. Nowadays, it has become linked with rituals and decisions involving dropping what is redundant, as a snake sheds its skin. It is perfect for regeneration and helps the user to focus on new objectives. Ruled by Mercury

How to Use Herbs in my Magical Workings?

Thyme

Thyme brings excellent health, recovers memory and mental abilities, and has strong antiseptic properties. It is said to aid recall of the past and allows glimpses into the future; to give courage and strength.

Added to your sleep pillow, it will keep away bad dreams and will bring happy prophetic ones. Ruled by Venus

Valerian

Valerian is a relaxant, decreases tension, anxiety, stress-related conditions, and insomnia. It gives effective pain relief for tension-related diseases, including migraines.

As an herb of reconciliation, it can be used in poppets, which are tied together to bring harmony to a relationship or reunite people separated by anger or circumstances. It was utilized by the Ancient Greeks to keep away all harm.

Nowadays, it is still regarded as an herb of peace and protection. Ruled by Venus

Vervain

Vervain is a nervous system's natural strengthener, reducing tension and the effects of stress. It relieves depression, particularly after an illness. It offers protection against all negativity.

A sachet hung above a toddler's bed drives away nightmares. Vervain brings happiness and intelligence to the very young. A sprig can be exchanged with a friend or lover as a promise of honesty at all times. Ruled by Venus

How to Use Herbs in my Magical Workings?

Yarrow

Yarrow slows the heartbeat, lowers blood pressure, speeds the healing of wounds, and lessens fevers. Yarrow is declared as an herb of love, keeping a couple together for at least seven years. The herb should be given to newly-weds and used in any love charms.

The married couples should store the herb in a different sachet and replace it just before seven years is over. They should replace it every seven years throughout their married life, making it into a ceremony of vow renewal. It also repels hostility and banishes fear. Ruled by Venus

How to Use Herbs in my Magical Workings?

Zodiac Signs in Spell Working

Notes for Chapter 4

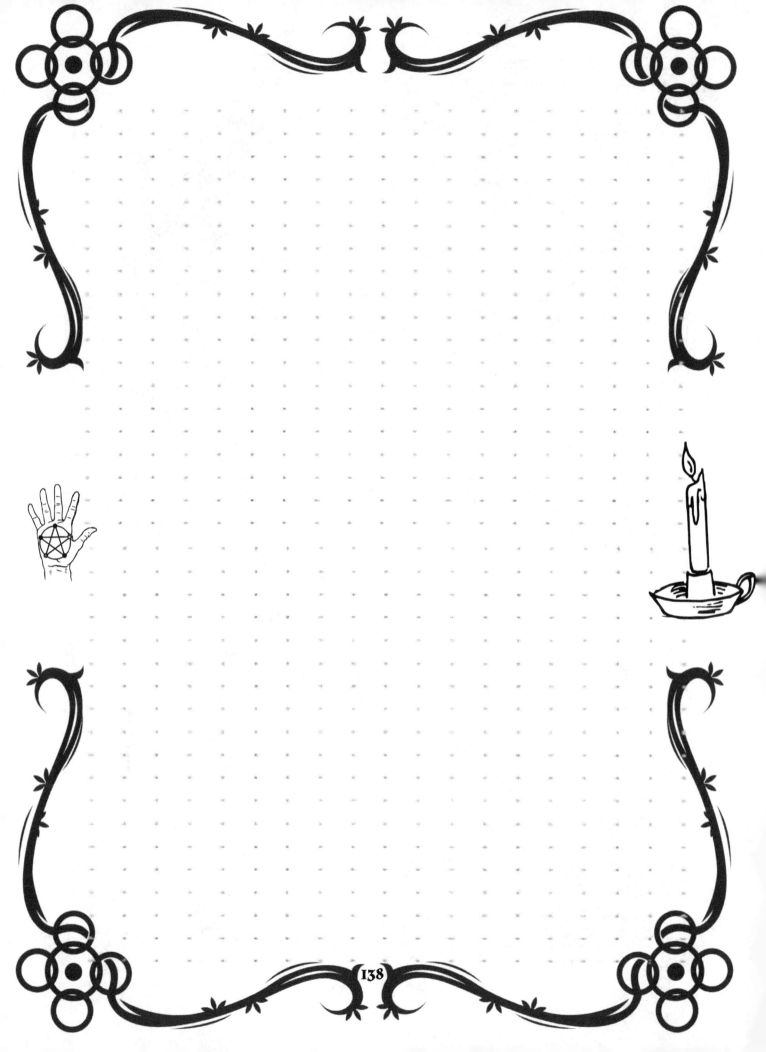

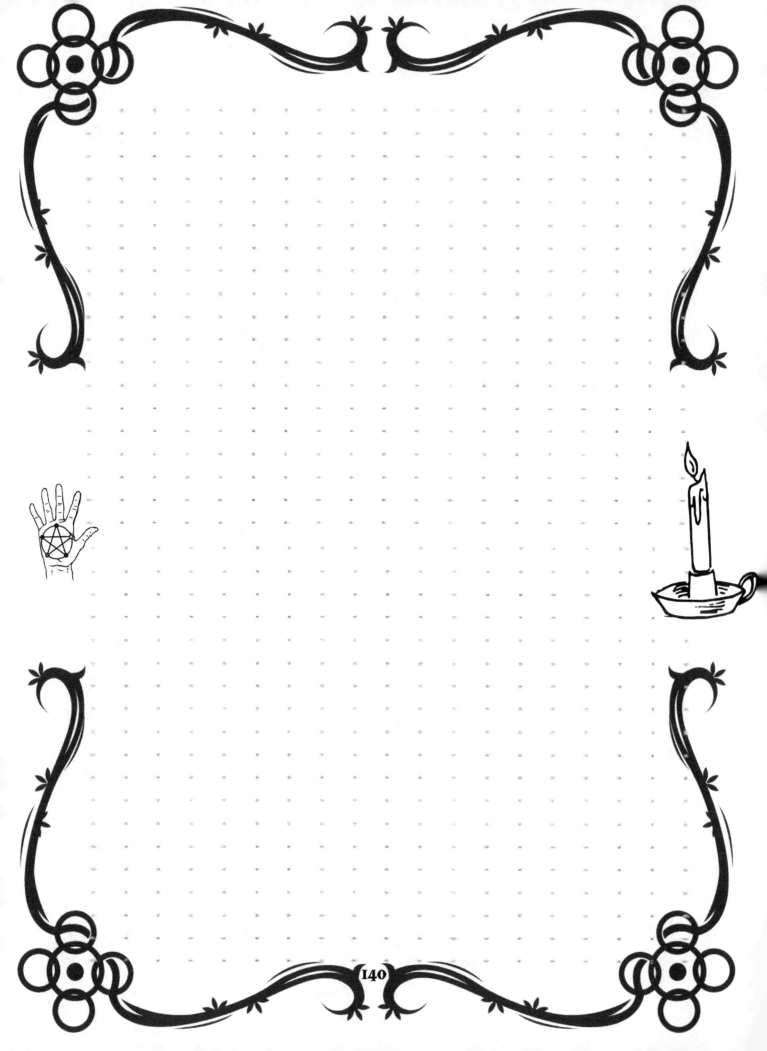

Aries

Aries is a Fire sign, and it is ruled by Mars. They are youthful and independent types, and can accomplish a lot on their own, when they are patient and motivated enough. They prefer to take things into their own hands more often than asking for help. Their energy is pure and bright like a flame, but like all flames they eventually burn out and need to be rekindled. Working with a coven can give Aries an outside perspective from their own and can help keep them motivated.

Spirit: Adventurous, courageous

Objectives: To plan and rule

Ego: Dominating, challenging

Personality: Impulsive, friendly, aggressive

Key Word: Activity

Key Phrase: I am

Empowerment Colors: Reds, Scarlet

Moderating Colors: Indigo

Birthstones - Ruby Garnet, Diamond

Tarot cards: The Emperor, 2, 3 & 4 of Wands

Gender – Masculine

Symbol – Ram,

Sigil: Ram's horns

Body part – Head & Face

Planet – Mars

Element – Fire

Quality – Cardinal

Fortunate Metal: Copper

Natural House: The First

Season: Spring,

Day: Tuesday,

Number: 9

Star Stone - Diamond, Bloodstone

Natural Phenomena - Thunder & Lightning

My Favorite Mantra

Aries (March 20 - April 20)

Be the best version of yourself and shine with these mantras. Focus on your strengths and make the best of the situations in life. Here are the mantras you should read, color, rewrite, and follow as per Aries zodiac sign.

- When I masterfully channel this fire into strength and strategy, I win!
- I am a warrior of bold love
- When I have an idea, I can achieve the goal!
- I slay my own ego to arise with greater courage and power!
- My fire is my most powerful tool!
- I am adventurous & courageous
- I'm not interested in the possibilities of defeat! They do not exist!
- I accept what is, I let go of what was, & I have faith in what could be!
- Patience, Patience!
- My heart will always lead me true.
- I give myself permission to slow down.
- If you have the idea, you can achieve the goal.
- We are not interested in the possibilities of defeat; they do not exist.

Which of these mantras resonates the most with you? Do you have your own personal mantra? Write it down!

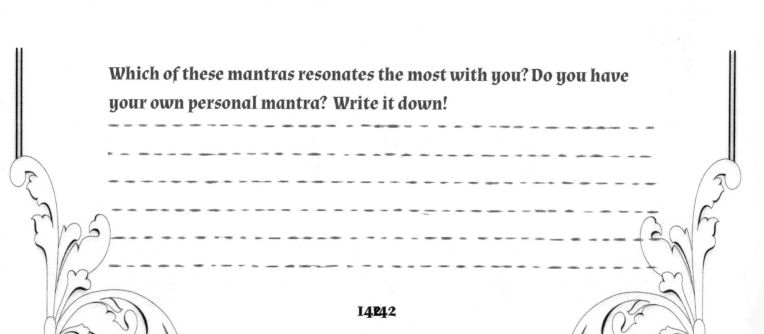

Notes

My Spiritual Practice in the Craft

TAURUS

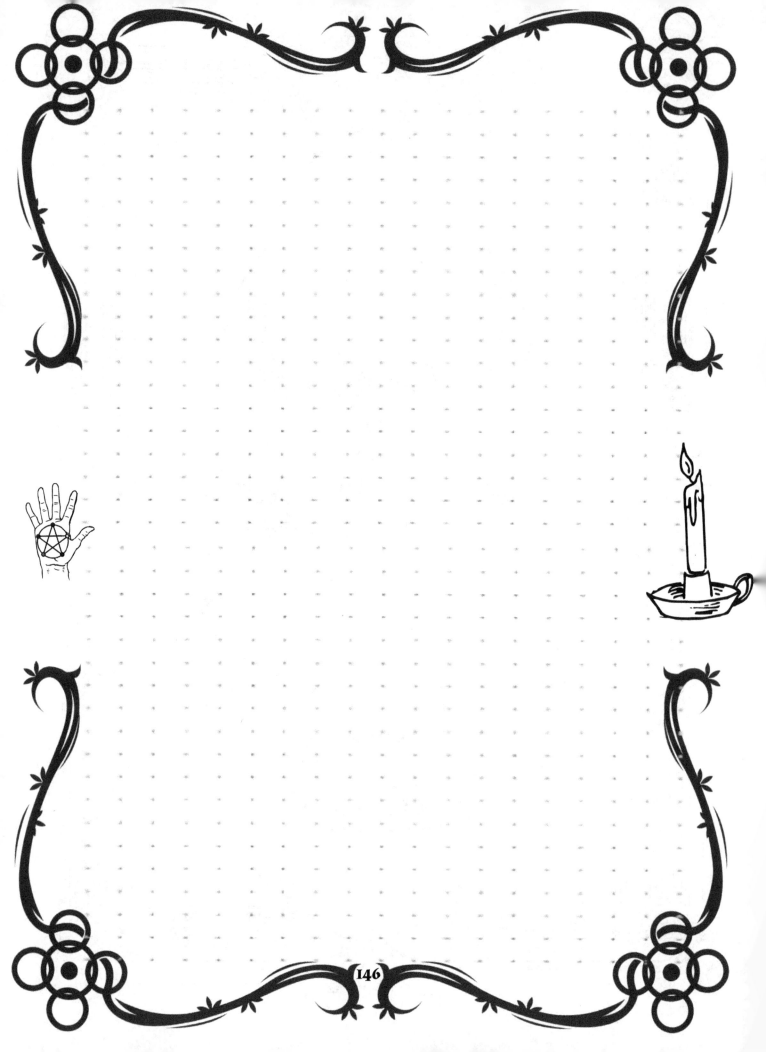

Taurus

Taurus is an Earth sign, and it is ruled by Venus. They are deeply rooted in the physical realm and are strongly driven by their desires. They instinctively know about the curative powers of nature and can act as a bridge to helping their fellow humans understand nature better.

Key Word: Stability

Key Phrase: I have

Spirit: Conservation, methodical, enjoy comfort

Objectives: To accumulate money

Ego: Affectionate, stubborn, competent

Personality: Indolent, voluptuous

Traditional Taurus Traits
Patient and reliable
Warm hearted and loving
Persistent and determined
Placid and security loving

Season: Spring,
Day: Friday,
Number: 6
Ruling Planet – Venus

Gender – Feminine
Symbol – Bull
Element – Earth
Metal: Copper
Star Stone - Emerald
Birthstone - Blue (Star) Sapphire
Body part – Shoulders, Arms
Empowerment Colors: Pale Blue, Green
Moderating Colors: Yellow
Quality – Kerubic (Fixed)
Natural House: The Second
Natural Phenomena - Volcanic Eruption
Tarot cards: The Hierophant, 5, 6 & 7 of Pentacles

My Favorite Mantra

Taurus (April 20 to May 20)

Be the best version of yourself and shine with these mantras. Focus on your strengths and make the best of the situations in life. Here are the mantras you should read, color, rewrite, and follow as per Taurus zodiac sign.

- My actions create a lot of value for others
- Nothing worth having comes easy!
- I am prosperous, and I am grateful for all the good things in my life!
- My loving connections are peaceful, loyal, and enduring!
- I am a force of peace & I enjoy the peace I extend!
- My heart's desire lies in protecting those I love!
- I am strong enough to endure change.
- I am prepared for the challenges of the day.
- When I don't like either of two paths, I make a new one!
- I possess a goldmine of divine light within me!
- I rise to new levels of valor with resilience & dignity!

Which of these mantras resonates the most with you? Do you have your own personal mantra? Write it down!

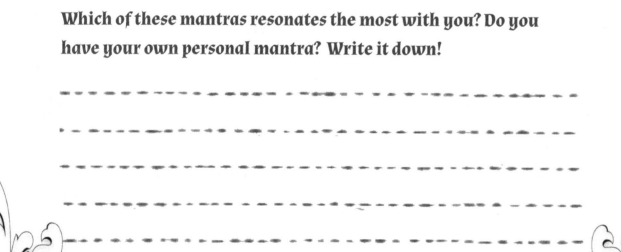

Notes

My Spiritual Practice in the Craft

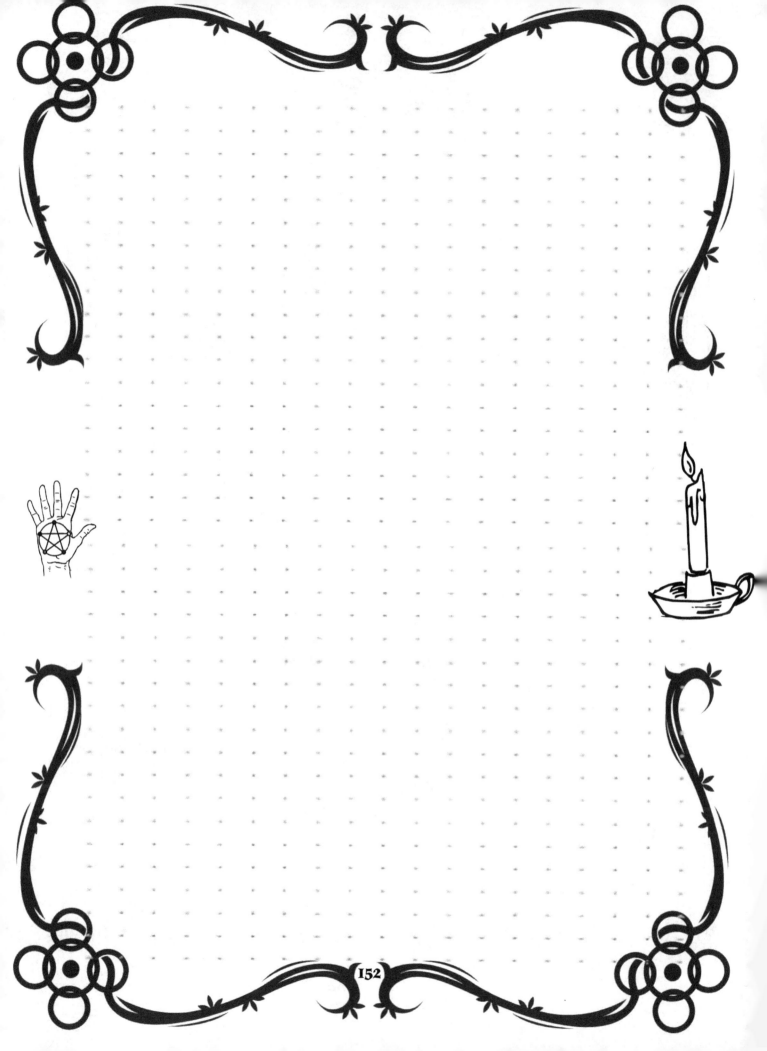

Gemini

Gemini is an Air sign, ruled by Mercury. Geminis perceive the world in a mental and visual way, and their perception is the most advanced of all signs. They are "I have to see it to believe it" types, and when they can stay focused long enough, they can visualize possibilities and outcomes quite accurately in order to manifest what they want in life.

Spirit: To investigate
Objectives: To advance by communications
Ego: Curious, imaginative
Personality: Talkative, restless
Traditional Gemini Traits
Adaptable and versatile
Communicative and witty
Intellectual and eloquent
Youthful and lively
Key Word: Versatility
Key Phrase: I think
Natural Phenomena - Hurricane
Tarot cards: The Lovers, 8, 9 & 10 of Swords

Ruler - Mercury
Gender – Masculine
Metal: Mercury
Quality – Mutable
Natural House: The Third
Symbol – Twins
Body part – Lungs
Element – Air
Empowerment Colours - Blue, slate, violet
Moderating Colors: Orange, soft browns
Star Stone - Moss Agate, Alexandrite
Birthstones - Agate, Carnelian
Season: Spring
Day: Wednesday **Num:** 5

My Favorite Mantra

Gemini (May 21 to June 20)

Be the best version of yourself and shine with these mantras. Focus on your strengths and make the best of the situations in life. Here are the mantras you should read, color, rewrite, and follow as per Gemini zodiac sign.

- I am most alive when I am learning something new
- Everything in life is working out for my highest good
- I will make room for honesty!
- I am a person of great value!
- All my dreams have come true
- I constantly think uplifting thoughts
- I am present and feel tremendous joy at this moment
- Each day I discover exciting, promising, and interesting new paths to travel
- I am happy performing random acts of kindness, compassion, love & happiness
- I truly love the person that I am
- Accept what is, let go of what was, and have faith in what could be!
- If it is not right, do not do it, if it is not true, do not say it!

Which of these mantras resonates the most with you? Do you have your own personal mantra? Write it down!

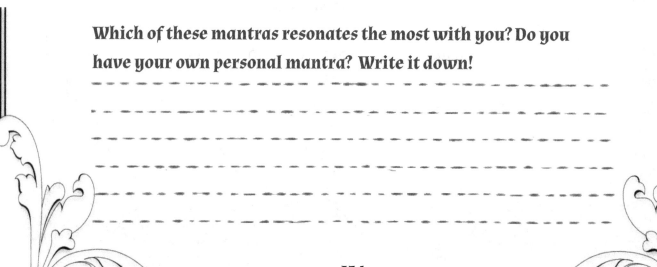

Notes

My Spiritual Practice in the Craft

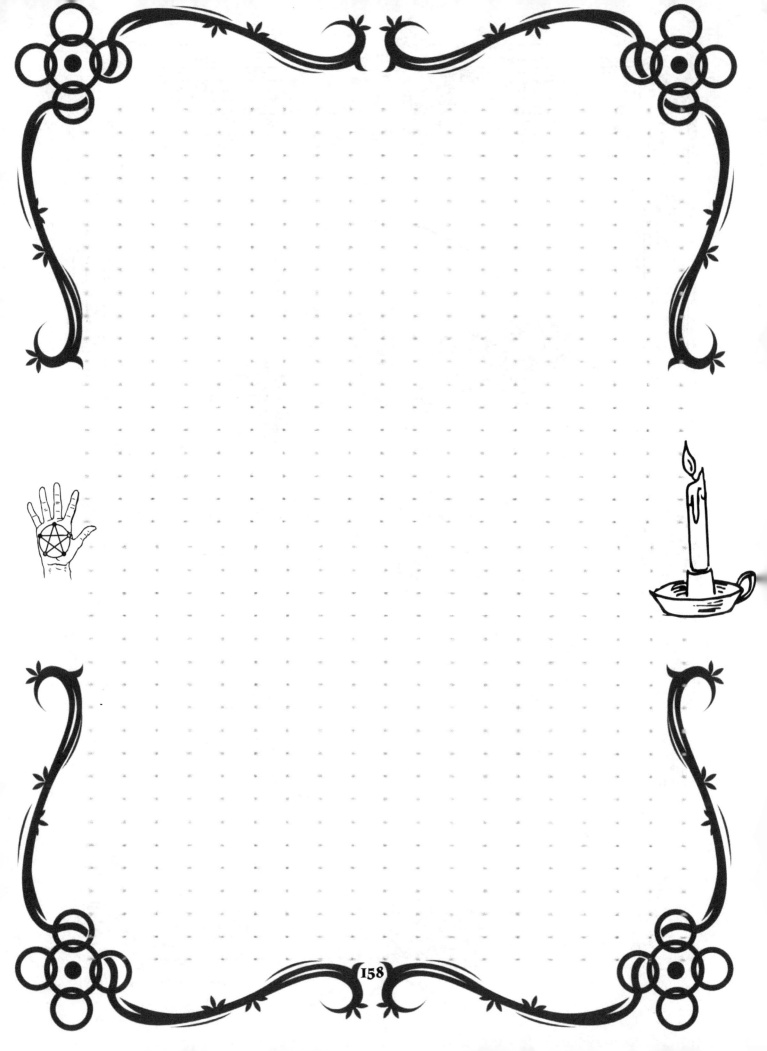

Cancer

Cancer is a Water sign, and it is ruled by the Moon. They are sensitive, emotionally caring, and are incredibly motherly. They are highly connected to the rhythms of the moon, and can be powerful healers and conductors of feminine energy. The Cancer sign is about fertility, protection, and nurturing. The attributes of Cancer are comforting, passionate, and empathetic.

Spirit: To win wealth and honors

Ego: Family oriented, unassuming, quiet

Personality: Sensitive, moody

Traditional Cancer Traits
Emotional and loving
Intuitive and imaginative
Shrewd and cautious
Protective and sympathetic

Key Word: Devotion

Key Phrase: I feel

Number: 2

Natural Phenomena - Maelstrom

Tarot cards: The Chariot, 2, 3 & 4 of Cups

Metal: Silver

Gender – Feminine

Symbol – Crab

Planet – The Moon

Quality – Cardinal

Natural House: The Fourth

Element – Water

Empowerment Colours - White, Silver

Moderating Colors: Violet

Star Stone - Pearl

Birthstones - Beryl, Moonstone, Pearl

Medical astrology – Breast and Stomach

Season: Summer,

Day: Monday,

My Favorite Mantra

Cancer (June 21 to July 22)

Be the best version of yourself and shine with these mantras. Focus on your strengths and make the best of the situations in life. Here are the mantras you should read, color, rewrite, and follow as per Gemini zodiac sign.

- I am at home in the world!
- The universe has my back and I have control over what I want
- I feel everything with pride!
- I am an unstoppable force of bold love
- I'm a survivor and can transform my vulnerability into personal power!
- My future is bright, and I am incredibly thankful for it
- I am the generator of my own abundance when I tap into my special gifts and express them confidently
- I can change the world and shift paradigms!
- I release all my negative thoughts about money and allow financial abundance to enter my life!
- I am more than I seem to be, and within me are all the powers of the Universe
- I am in possession of a healthy body and a healthy mind!
- Never let your emotions overpower your intelligence!

Which of these mantras resonates the most with you? Do you have your own personal mantra? Write it down!

Notes

My Spiritual Practice in the Craft

LEO

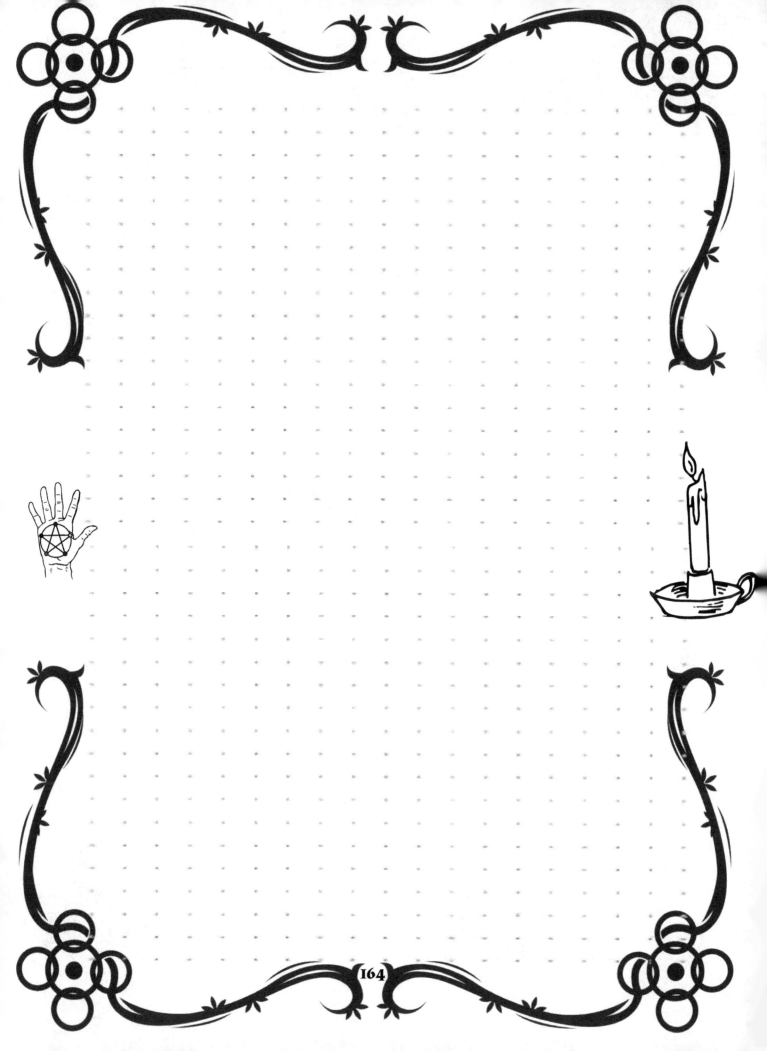

Leo

Leo is a Fire sign, and is ruled by the Sun. They perceive the world through their image, body movements, and their gut instincts. They tend to think that life is one big stage for them to perform and shine their light on in whatever way they want. They tend to be on the constant search for things and people in life that bring them excitement and allow for their passionate side to be expressed.

Spirit: To rule

Ego: Egotistical, optimistic, brave

Personality: Generous, dramatic, arrogant

Traditional Leo Traits

Generous and warm hearted

Creative and enthusiastic

Broad-minded and expansive

Faithful and loving

On the dark side....

Pompous and patronizing

Bossy and interfering

Dogmatic and intolerant

Key Word: Magnetism

Key Phrase: I will

Tarot cards: Strength (Lust), 5, 6 & 7 of Wands

Colours - Yellow, Orange, Gold

Star Stone - Ruby

Birthstones - Amber, Citrine, Diamond

Natural Phenomena - Solar Flare

Season: Summer,

Day: Sunday,

Number: 1

Gender – Masculine

Metal: Gold

Symbol – Lion

Body part – Heart

Planet – The Sun

Quality – Kerubic(Fixed)

Natural House: The Fifth

Element – Fire

My Favorite Mantra

Leo (July 23 to August 22)

Be the best version of yourself and shine with these mantras. Focus on your strengths and make the best of the situations in life. Here are the mantras you should read, color, rewrite, and follow as per Leo zodiac sign.

- I am so happy and grateful because I get to live the life of my dreams
- It's not all about me!
- It's Okay to Just Be
- I am confident in my own worth.
- I win when I follow my joy.
- I let go of ego and embrace what life throws at me.
- My inner royalty is ready to emerge and receive its due admiration
- My heart is renewing to the innocence of the divine child – radiant, joyful and pure!
- I am capable of manifesting maximum strength and health
- I deserve to be prosperous & to have an abundance of money in my bank account
- I decide to make my life a masterpiece worth remembering!
- Success is naturally & effortlessly drawn to me in all areas of my life
- I love money and all the things that it lets me accomplish

Which of these mantras resonates the most with you? Do you have your own personal mantra? Write it down!

Notes

My Spiritual Practice in the Craft

VIRGO

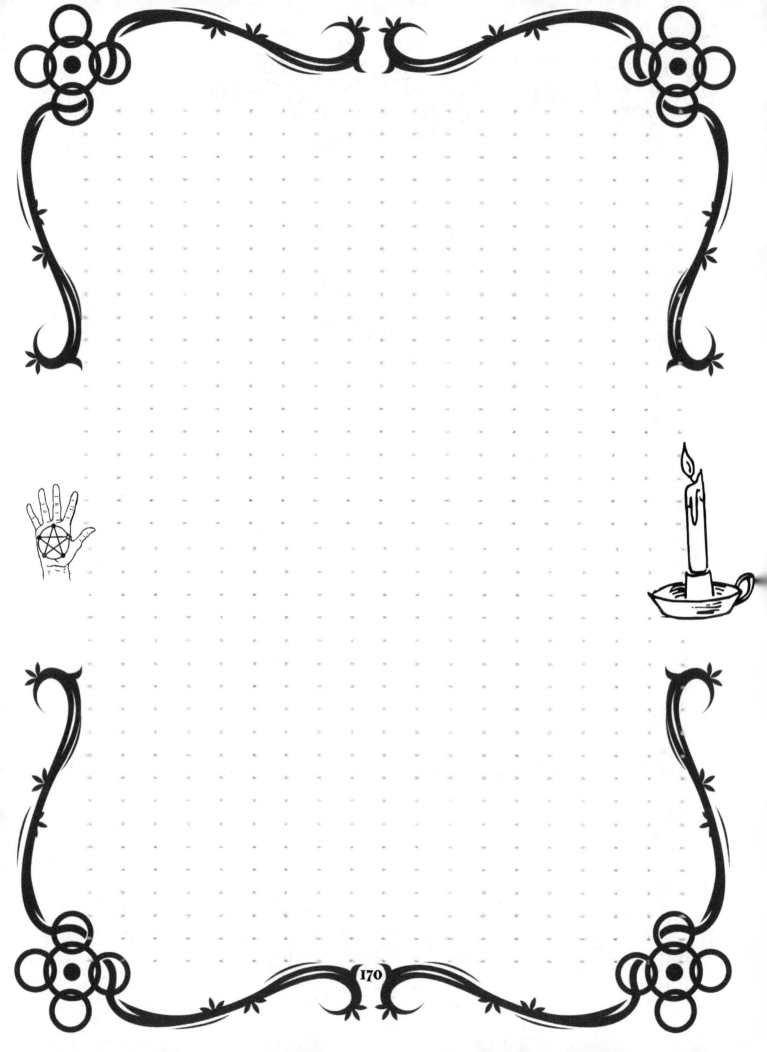

Virgo

Virgo is an Earth sign, and is ruled by Mercury. They are practical, down to earth people, preferring the simpler things in life. They are highly connected to nature, and they have a natural gift for working with plants. They tend to notice the subtlest of changes around them, and because of this sensitivity, they make natural-born healers and herbalists.

Spirit: To follow opportunity and serve

Ego: Analytical, critical, detail oriented

Personality: Fault finding, timid, self-possessed, cold

Traditional Virgo Traits

Modest and shy

Meticulous and reliable

Practical and diligent

Intelligent and analytical

On the dark side....

Fussy and a worrier

Over critical and harsh

Perfectionist and conservative

Key Word: Practicality

Key Phrase: I analyze

Element – Earth

Ruler - Mercury

Colours - Navy Blue, Gray

Star Stone -Sardonyx

Birthstones - Agate, sapphire

Season: Summer,

Day: Wednesday,

Number: 5

Metal: Mercury

Natural Phenomena - Earthquake

Gender – Feminine

Symbol – The Virgin

Body part – Stomach and Bowels

Quality – Mutable

Natural House: The Sixth

Tarot cards: The Hermit, 8, 9 & 10 of Pentacles

My Favorite Mantra

Virgo (August 23 to September 22)

Be the best version of yourself and shine with these mantras. Focus on your strengths and make the best of the situations in life. Here are the mantras you should read, color, rewrite, and follow as per Virgo zodiac sign.

- I am fit, energetic, attractive & healthy!
- My future is bright, and I am incredibly thankful for it!
- I am the creator of my life!
- I am happy & always have control over how I feel!
- I find it easy and effortless to be optimistic every day
- I am more than I seem to be, & within me are all the powers of the Universe
- I embody my creative power, I see beyond the surface and allow no one to manipulate me
- I am a do-er! I will take action & get things accomplished
- I silence my inner critic!
- The world needs my skills
- I'm devoted to the mastery of myself
- I am enough!

Which of these mantras resonates the most with you? Do you have your own personal mantra? Write it down!

Notes

My Spiritual Practice in the Craft

LIBRA

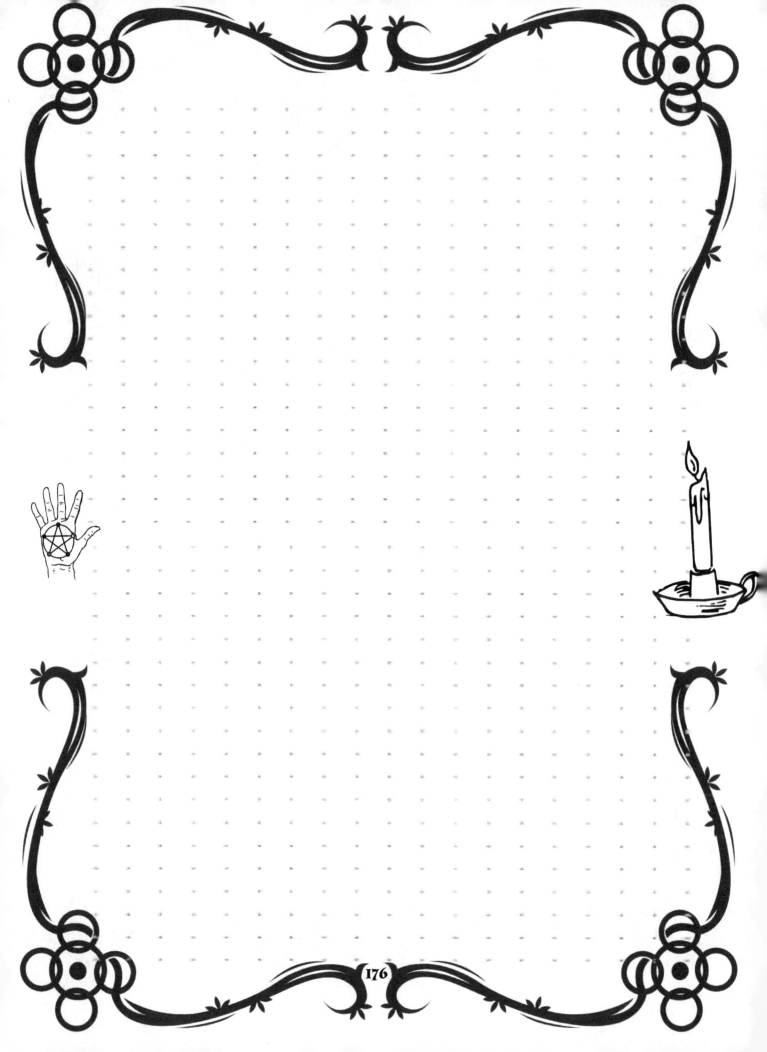

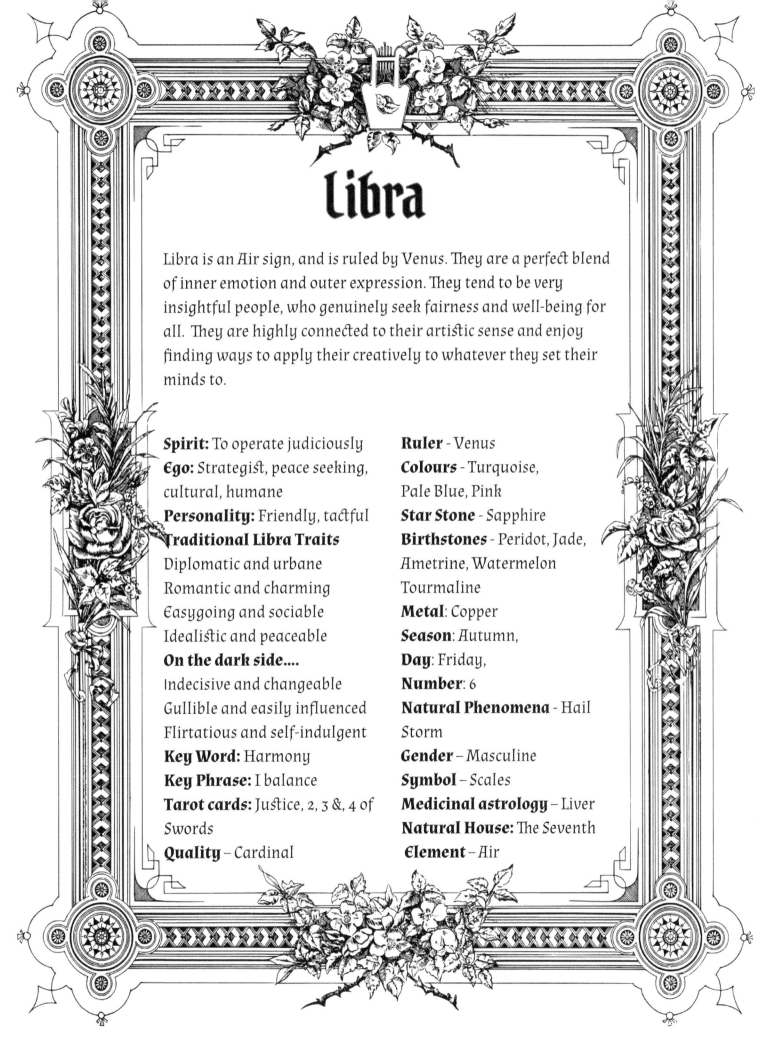

Libra

Libra is an Air sign, and is ruled by Venus. They are a perfect blend of inner emotion and outer expression. They tend to be very insightful people, who genuinely seek fairness and well-being for all. They are highly connected to their artistic sense and enjoy finding ways to apply their creatively to whatever they set their minds to.

Spirit: To operate judiciously

Ego: Strategist, peace seeking, cultural, humane

Personality: Friendly, tactful

Traditional Libra Traits

Diplomatic and urbane
Romantic and charming
Easygoing and sociable
Idealistic and peaceable

On the dark side....

Indecisive and changeable
Gullible and easily influenced
Flirtatious and self-indulgent

Key Word: Harmony

Key Phrase: I balance

Tarot cards: Justice, 2, 3 &, 4 of Swords

Quality – Cardinal

Ruler - Venus

Colours - Turquoise, Pale Blue, Pink

Star Stone - Sapphire

Birthstones - Peridot, Jade, Ametrine, Watermelon Tourmaline

Metal: Copper

Season: Autumn,

Day: Friday,

Number: 6

Natural Phenomena - Hail Storm

Gender – Masculine

Symbol – Scales

Medicinal astrology – Liver

Natural House: The Seventh

Element – Air

My Favorite Mantra

Libra (September 23 to October 22)

Be the best version of yourself and shine with these mantras. Focus on your strengths and make the best of the situations in life. Here are the mantras you should read, color, rewrite, and follow as per Libra zodiac sign.

- I make positive choices for myself
- I release old grudges with grace!
- I rise to my responsibility as a heart-centered leader and mother-protector!
- I balance kindness with assertiveness to achieve creative potential in partnership!
- Follow your heart but take your brain with you!
- I am eternally grateful for the abundance in my life!
- I attract powerful and successful people who understand, motivate, and inspire me daily!
- As I take bold action the future looks bright with possibility!
- Follow your heart but take your brain with you

Which of these mantras resonates the most with you? Do you have your own personal mantra? Write it down!

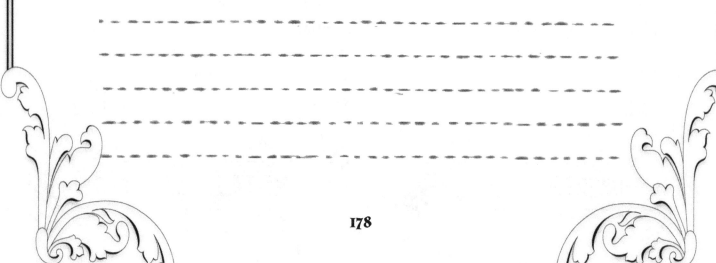

178

Notes

My Spiritual Practice in the Craft

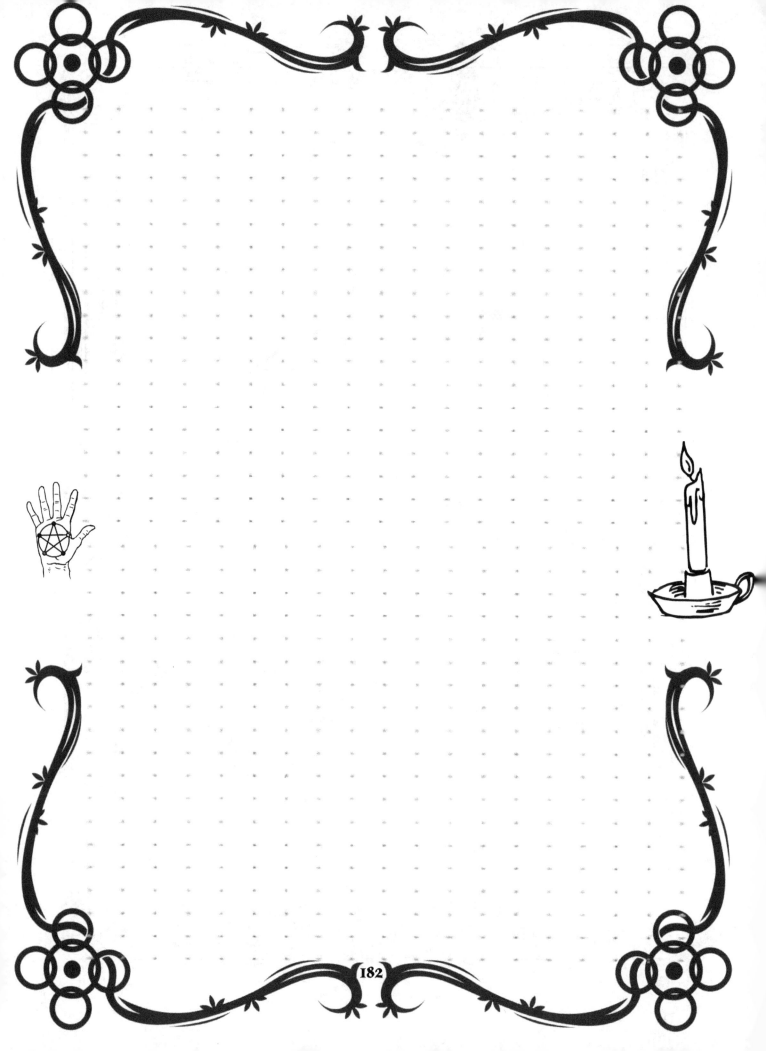

Scorpio

Scorpio is a Water sign, and is ruled by Pluto. They are highly psychic, intuitive, and sexual people. Their intuition is intense, and tends to guide most of their actions, and because of this they have a natural gift for reading situations and people accurately.

Spirit: To penetrate the secrets of nature

Ego: Shrewd, perceptive, strong willed, passionate

Personality: Secretive, vengeful, ardent

Traditional Scorpio Traits
Determined and forceful
Emotional and intuitive
Powerful and passionate
Exciting and magnetic

On the dark side....
Jealous and resentful

Key Word: Intensity

Key Phrase: I desire

Element – Water

Tarot cards: Death, 5, 6 & 7 of Cups

Rulers / Planets - Pluto, Mars, Lilith

Colors - Black, Scarlet, Dark Red

Star Stone - Opal

Birthstones - Diamond, Obsidian

Metal: Iron

Season: Autumn,

Day: Tuesday,

Number: 9

Gender – Feminine

Symbol – Scorpion

Natural Phenomena - Tsunami

Body part – Sex Organs, Intestines

Quality – Kerubic (Fixed)

Natural House: The Eighth

My Favorite Mantra

Scorpio (October 23 to November 21)

Be the best version of yourself and shine with these mantras. Focus on your strengths and make the best of the situations in life. Here are the mantras you should read, color, rewrite, and follow as per Scorpio zodiac sign.

- I open my heart and mind & reveal my authentic self!
- I will allow myself to sink into vulnerability!
- My capacity for transformation is my greatest strength!
- My confidence is radiant, powerful and magnetic for all to witness
- I I allow no one else to define me, my beliefs or my morality
- I won't hide
- I have all that I need!
- I stop being afraid of what could go wrong, I think about what could go right!
- Kill them with kindness and bury them with a smile!
- Betrayal is met with dragonfire!
- As I master myself through discipline and duty, my destiny is transformed!

Which of these mantras resonates the most with you? Do you have your own personal mantra? Write it down!

Notes

My Spiritual Practice in the Craft

SAGGITARIUS

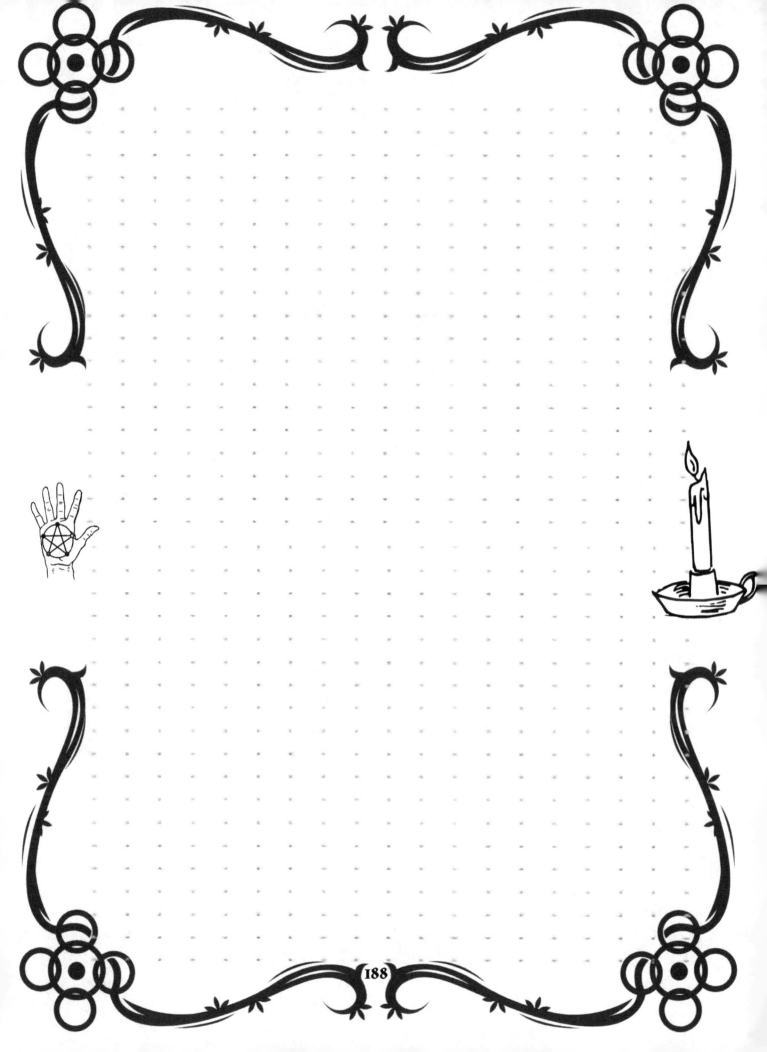

Sagittarius

Sagittarius is a Fire sign, and is ruled by Jupiter. They are the eternal students of life, are highly philosophical and like to travel because they enjoy learning from other traditions and cultures.

Spirit: Meeting competition

Ego: Independent, studious, intuitive, free-thinking

Personality: Restless, enterprising, over-confident

Traditional Sagittarius Traits

Optimistic and freedom-loving
Jovial and good-humoured
Honest and straightforward
Intellectual and philosophical

On the dark side....

Blindly optimistic and careless
Irresponsible and superficial
Tactless and restless.

Key Word: Visualization

Key Phrase: I understand

Element – Fire

Ruler - Jupiter

Colors - Blue, Purple, Striped Patterns

Star Stone - Topaz

Birthstones - Sapphire, Turquoise

Metal: Tin

Season: Autumn,

Day: Thursday,

Number: 3

Natural Phenomena - Fire Storm

Gender – Masculine

Symbol – Archer

Body part – Thighs and Hips

Quality – Mutable

Natural House: The Ninth

Tarot cards: Temperance (Art), 8, 9, 10 of Wands

My Favorite Mantra

Sagittarius (November 22 – December 21)

Be the best version of yourself and shine with these mantras. Focus on your strengths and make the best of the situations in life. Here are the mantras you should read, color, rewrite, and follow as per Sagittarius zodiac sign.

- I can easily create a life I love
- Happiness is my natural state of being
- I am developing new, positive habits that serve my goals!
- I am my own guru!
- I am worthy of being healthy!
- I am in control of my state at all times
- I feel grateful for the money I have!
- I find it easy and effortless to be optimistic every day
- I am more than I seem to be, within me are all the Powers of the Universe!
- I can turn big ideas into action!
- I am destined for success and greatness
- I recognize every opportunity that knocks on my door and
- seizes it immediately

Which of these mantras resonates the most with you? Do you have your own personal mantra? Write it down!

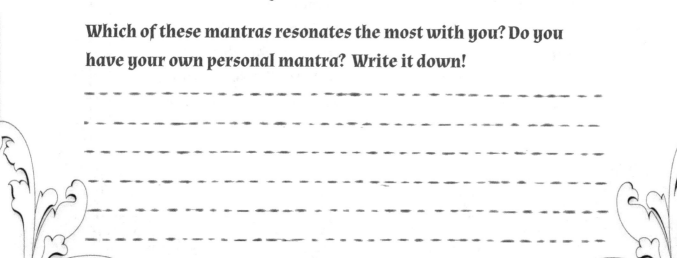

Notes

My Spiritual Practice in the Craft

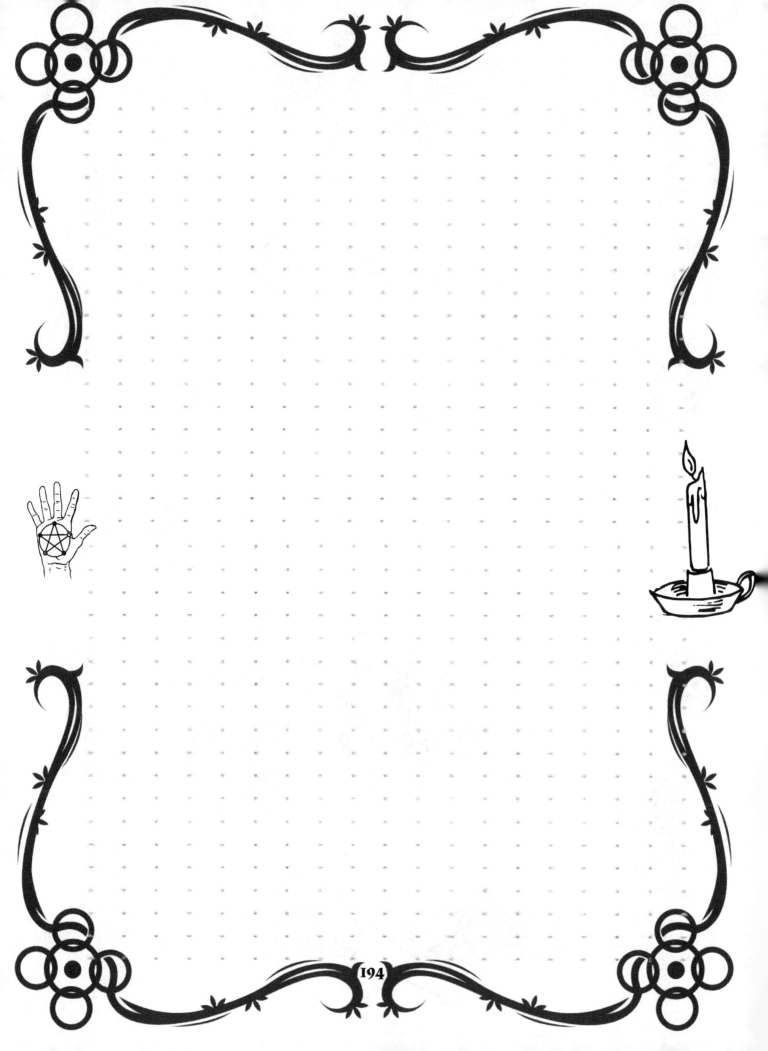

Capricorn

Capricorn is an Earth sign, and is ruled by Saturn. They are mountain climbers of the peaks of life. They are career-oriented, and enjoy challenges. They are not scared to put in the hard work to achieve what they want, and will do what it takes to get to the top of the mountains of their goals.

Spirit: To persevere and attain goals

Ego: Methodical, cautious, practical, ambitious

Personality: Pessimistic, miserly, ruthless

Traditional Capricorn Traits

Practical and prudent

Ambitious and disciplined

Patient and careful

Humorous and reserved

On the dark side….

Pessimistic and fatalistic

Miserly and grudging.

Key Word: Ambition

Key Phrase: I use

Natural House: The Tenth

Element – Earth

Ruler - Saturn

Colors - Black, Brown

Star Stone - Black Diamond, Onyx

Birthstones - Garnet, Jet, Onyx

Metal: Lead

Season: Winter,

Day: Saturday,

Number: 8

Gender – Feminine

Symbol – Goat

Natural Phenomena - Landslide

Body part – Genitals, Knees and Bones

Quality – Cardinal

Tarot cards: The Devil, 2, 3 & 4 of Pentacles

My Favorite Mantra

Capricorn (December 22 to January 19)

Be the best version of yourself and shine with these mantras. Focus on your strengths and make the best of the situations in life. Here are the mantras you should read, color, rewrite, and follow as per Capricorn zodiac sign.

- I deserve to be happy!
- I trust myself because my inner wisdom knows the truth!
- I am sovereign to my own dignified soul
- Deep and true intimacy takes bold and strategic courage
- An awakening is stirring at the very fundamental levels of my life
- I Don't Need to Do It All
- Worrying will never change the outcome
- I know when to walk away!
- I honor my desire to bond and love, but cannot be possessed!
- When the ground shifts beneath my feet, I find the inner orientation to steady myself and thrive!
- I am comfortable in my own skin even outside my comfort zone!
- I succeed when I treat myself and others with kindness!

Which of these mantras resonates the most with you? Do you have your own personal mantra? Write it down!

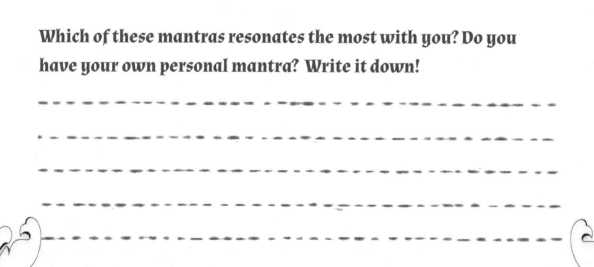

Notes

My Spiritual Practice in the Craft

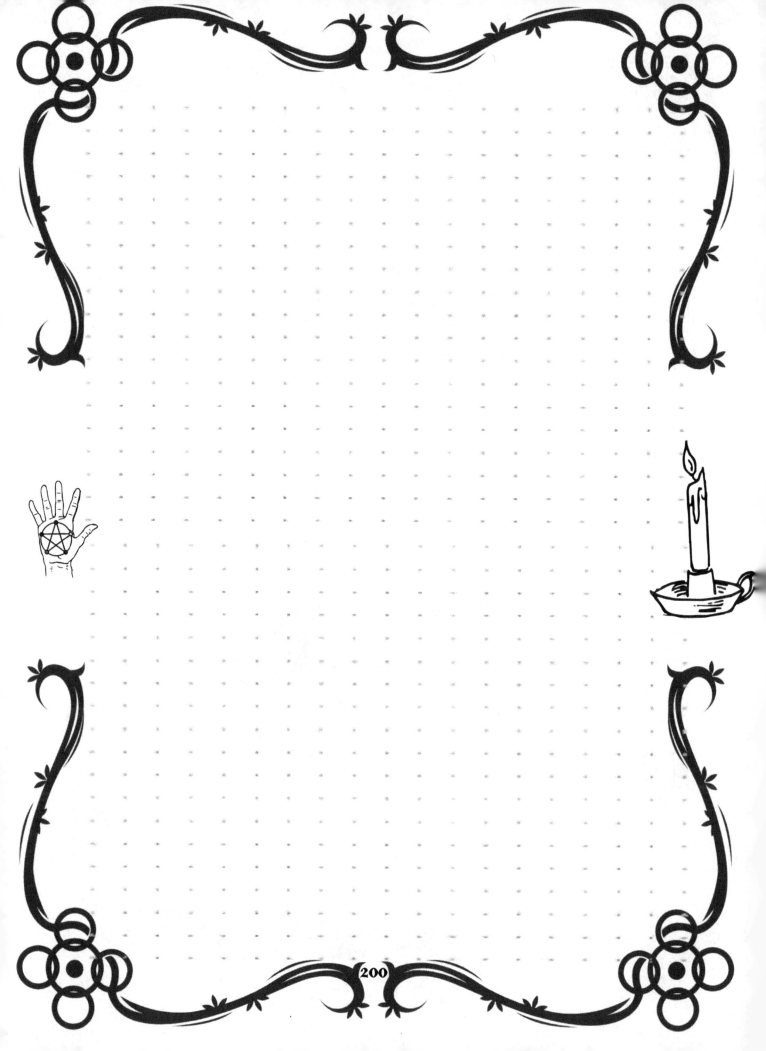

Aquarius

Aquarius is an Air sign, and is ruled by Uranus. They perceive the world through their minds, but their ideals are what drive them. They are natural-born humanitarians and want to see the betterment of humanity and help to bring it about.

Spirit: To spread philosophical thought

Ego: Aesthetic, altruistic, revolutionary, unconventional

Personality: Stubborn, independent, eccentric

Traditional Aquarius Traits
Friendly and humanitarian
Honest and loyal
Original and inventive
Independent and intellectual

On the dark side....
Intractable and contrary
Perverse and unpredictable
Unemotional and detached

Key Word: Imagination

Key Phrase: I know

Natural House: The Eleventh

Element – Air

Ruler - Uranus, Saturn

Colors - White, Bright Blue, Magenta

Star Stone - Turquoise, Amethyst

Birthstones - Opal, Aquamarine

Metal: Uranium, Aluminum

Season: Winter,

Day: Saturday,

Number: 4

Natural Phenomena - Thunderstorm

Gender – Masculine

Symbol – Water Bearer

Body part – Kidneys, Bladder

Quality – Kerubic (Fixed)

Tarot cards: The Star, 5, 6 & 7 of Swords

My Favorite Mantra

Aquarius (January 20 to February 18)

Be the best version of yourself and shine with these mantras. Focus on your strengths and make the best of the situations in life. Here are the mantras you should read, color, rewrite, and follow as per Aquarius zodiac sign.

- I have the full power to lift myself and my spirits up
- whenever I desire!
- Each moment that I am alive, I become happier and happier with my life!
- My Uniqueness Is my Gift
- I am open to new ideas and new ways of thinking
- I will search for the good that comes even in bad situations!
- I will stop resigning to an isolated existence!
- It's time to allow myself to be truly seen and loved
- I shine as the architect of my heart's calling!
- As I investigate my own desires and responses, I find the answers to my relationship needs
- I am able to move past challenges and mistakes quickly and effortlessly!
- I am truly blessed and grateful to everyone who has touched my life and has made it worth living!
- I transform any obstacle into abundant opportunities

Which of these mantras resonates the most with you? Do you have your own personal mantra? Write it down!

Notes

My Spiritual Practice in the Craft

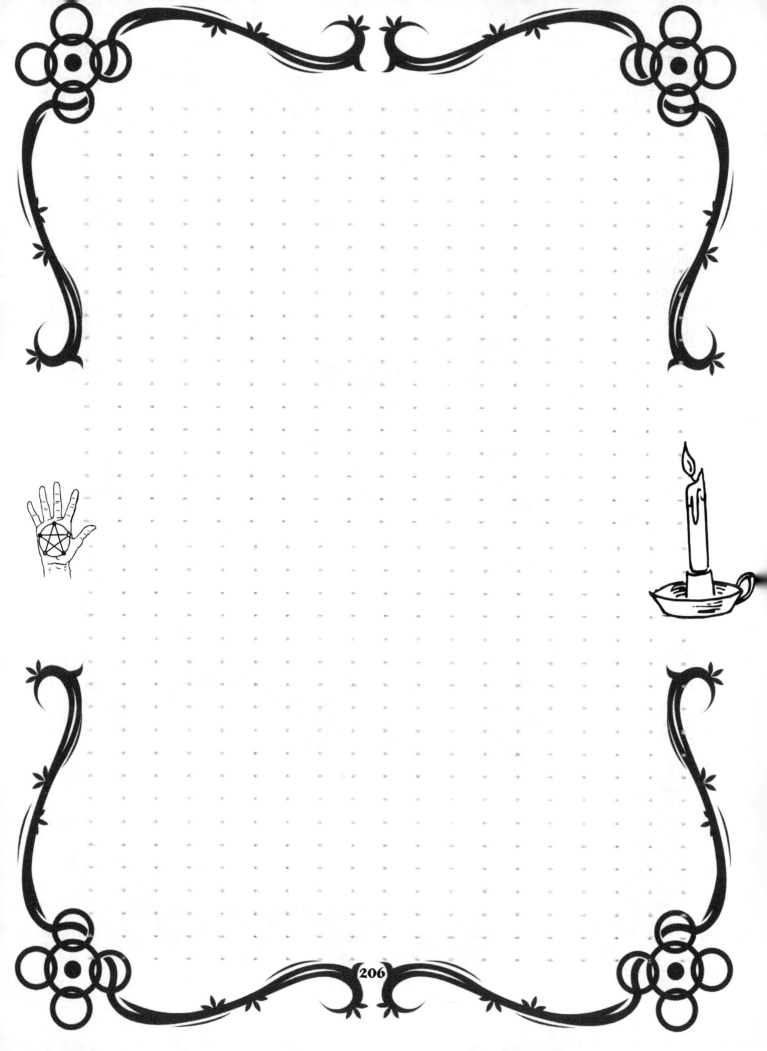

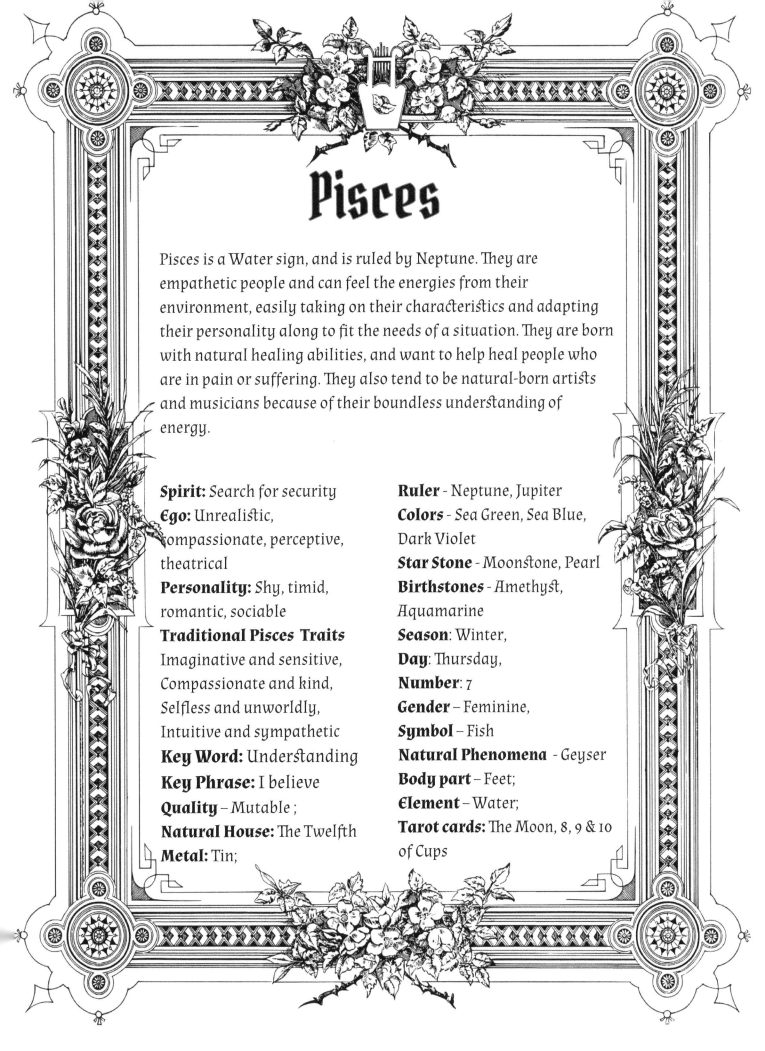

Pisces

Pisces is a Water sign, and is ruled by Neptune. They are empathetic people and can feel the energies from their environment, easily taking on their characteristics and adapting their personality along to fit the needs of a situation. They are born with natural healing abilities, and want to help heal people who are in pain or suffering. They also tend to be natural-born artists and musicians because of their boundless understanding of energy.

Spirit: Search for security

Ego: Unrealistic, compassionate, perceptive, theatrical

Personality: Shy, timid, romantic, sociable

Traditional Pisces Traits
Imaginative and sensitive, Compassionate and kind, Selfless and unworldly, Intuitive and sympathetic

Key Word: Understanding

Key Phrase: I believe

Quality – Mutable ;

Natural House: The Twelfth

Metal: Tin;

Ruler - Neptune, Jupiter

Colors - Sea Green, Sea Blue, Dark Violet

Star Stone - Moonstone, Pearl

Birthstones - Amethyst, Aquamarine

Season: Winter,

Day: Thursday,

Number: 7

Gender – Feminine,

Symbol – Fish

Natural Phenomena - Geyser

Body part – Feet;

Element – Water;

Tarot cards: The Moon, 8, 9 & 10 of Cups

My Favorite Mantra

Pisces (February 19 to March 20)

Be the best version of yourself and shine with these mantras. Focus on your strengths and make the best of the situations in life. Here are the mantras you should read, color, rewrite, and follow as per Pisces zodiac sign.

- All encounters have beauty if you look close enough
- Don't over-think, just let it go!
- I am a channel that love and insight flows through!
- I find it easy and effortless to be optimistic every day
- I matter! I am allowed to say 'No' to others and 'Yes' to myself!
- I dare to share my talents
- My actions create a lot of value for others!
- I can't save the world but I can heal the collective soul wounds
- I shine when I infuse my work with meaning and sacredness
- I honor my body, and I am surrounded by others who want me to be healthy!
- My heart contains a vast Universe of compassion
- The vision I have, creates a success, that surrounds me
- in my daily life!

Which of these mantras resonates the most with you? Do you have your own personal mantra? Write it down!

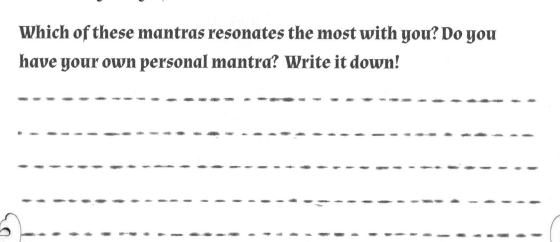

Notes

My Spiritual Practice in the Craft

Chapter 5

Magical Oils
and Their Uses

Notes for Chapter 5

A-C

Amber: Amber is the ideal scent for general relaxation or to achieve a pleasant environment in the room. The focus of Amber is happiness, love, and comfort. It is a beautiful scent, and it blends well with many settings. It is used frequently as therapeutic in healing and meditation and for emotional stability.

Benzoin: Benzoin reduces resentment, tension, stress, anger, frustrations and emotional pain. It undoubtedly increases self-confidence and attracts material and spiritual prosperity. It mixes very well with lavender, rose, and pine.

Bergamot: Bergamot soothes irritation and lifts depression or apathy, encouraging honest but gentle communication and the manifestation of a person's inner self and real potential. You can mix bergamot well with ylang-ylang and frankincense.

Cinnamon: It has a beautiful smell and is an essential part of many tasty recipes. Cinnamon is used as an incense for an aphrodisiac, money rituals, as increasing mental states, and healing. It is used incite high meditative moods and to purify a space.

Cedarwood: Cedarwood is a symbol of sexual and spiritual awakening after a period of loss or stagnation. This oil is excellent for meditation, and it is an oil of youthfulness and a long and happy life. It mixes wonderfully with rosemary, cypress, or Jumper.

Chamomile: Chamomile is well known as the oil of kindness and is suitable for children oil. It is useful for hyperactivity, general restlessness, and sleeplessness, beneficial for adults and kids. Chamomile mixes well with geranium, ylang-ylang, lavender, and lemon.

How to Use Herb Infused Oils in Magic

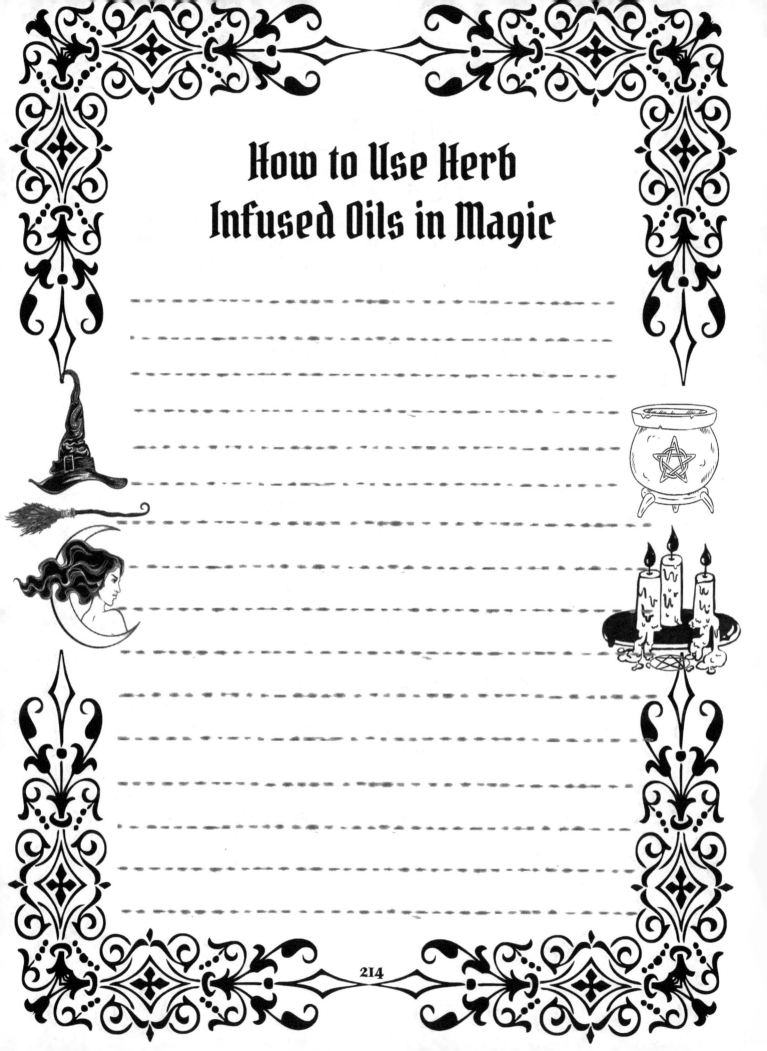

C, D, E

Clary sage: Clary sage drives away fears and nightmares and calms children and adults. It is also an oil of inspiration and positivity. When problems emerge, it replaces doubts with unconsidered options and with confidence that all will be well. It mixes well with Lavender, Ylang-ylang & rosemary.

Citronella: Citronella setting the boundaries of the individual and repelling those who would intrude on your professional or personal privacy. It also creates invisible fences around your home. Citronella improves mental sharpness and dispels inertia and exhaustion. It mixes well with jasmine and lavender.

Cypress: Cypress is the oil of consolation after grief or loss, bringing approval, healing, and it gives you the power to move forward. It promotes compassion and understanding of the distress of self and others. It mixes very well with geranium, lemon, and juniper.

Dragon's Blood: Dragon's Blood increases the potency of other scents used in your rituals. This scent is frequently used in protection, consecration, strength, and good luck rituals. It is also used in rituals that involve magic, love, or exorcism.

Eucalyptus: This oil drives out negativity and anger; it is for purification of mind, body, and soul. It repels planned the mental and psychic attack. Eucalyptus will provide the incentive for action and decisions, mainly when people or projects have reached some obstacles. This oil also offers increased concentration and a clear focus. It mixes well with Peppermint, Cedarwood, and clary sage.

How to Use Herb Infused Oils in Magic

F, G, J

Fennel: Fennel is the oil of perseverance, strength, and courage. It combines well with Chamomile and Eucalyptus.

Frangipani: Frangipani is also known as Plumeria and is cultivated in Hawaii. Used as an incense, it helps soothing vibrations and restores peace, harmony, and calm.

Frankincense: Frankincense is regarded as the noblest of oils. It is frequently used in ceremonies and formal celebrations throughout the centuries, respected in many cultures to be a gift from the gods with healing power. It offers you the courage to aim high, attract money, an abundance of all kinds, and success. Frankincense grants access to higher dimensions and contact with angels and spirits. Mixes well with myrrh, cypress, and sandalwood.

Geranium: Geranium is harmonizing oil, returning peace and wellbeing to your workplace and your home. It encourages positive, non-confrontational interactions, reconciling disagreements, and decreasing emotional coldness and indifference in encounters. It reduces depression doubts, tension, and despair, replacing them with optimism. It mixes well with Ylang-ylang, Lavender, Rose, Chamomile, Cedarwood, and most other oils.

Ginger: Ginger is an enhancer of passion, love, and money and inspires adventure and innovation. It mixes well with jasmine, Bergamot, Cedarwood.

Juniper: Juniper is cleansing and purifying the oil, guarding against hostility and eliminating what is redundant. It mixes well with cypress, rosemary, and frankincense.

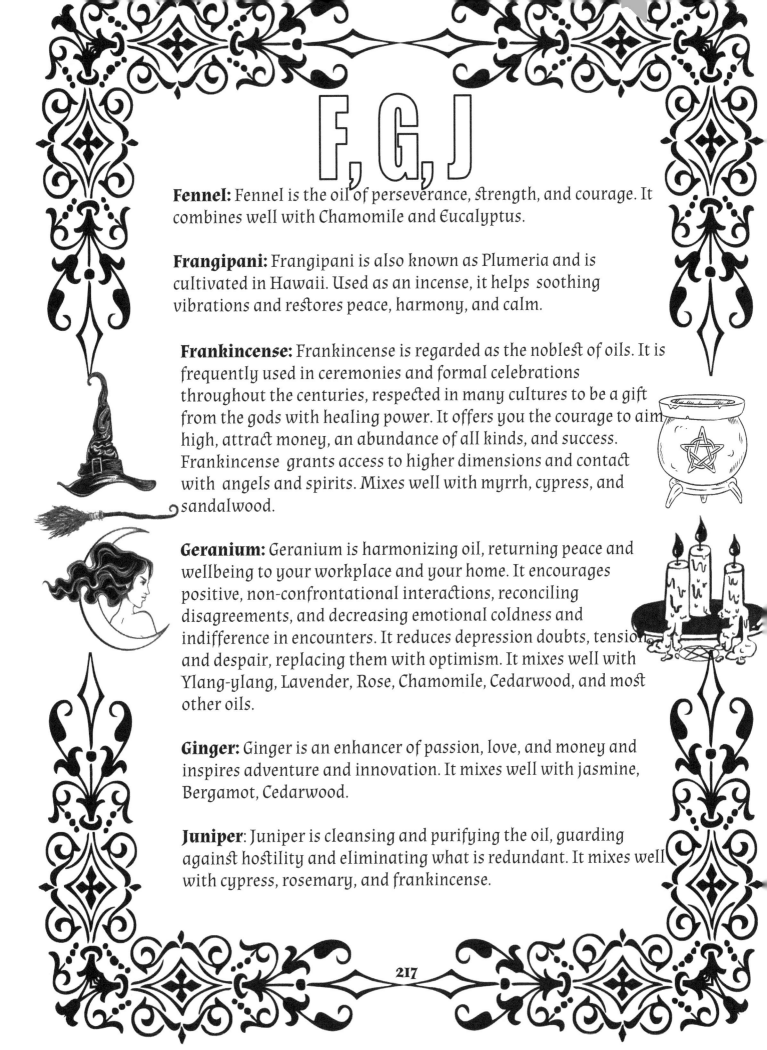

How to Use Herb Infused Oils in Magic

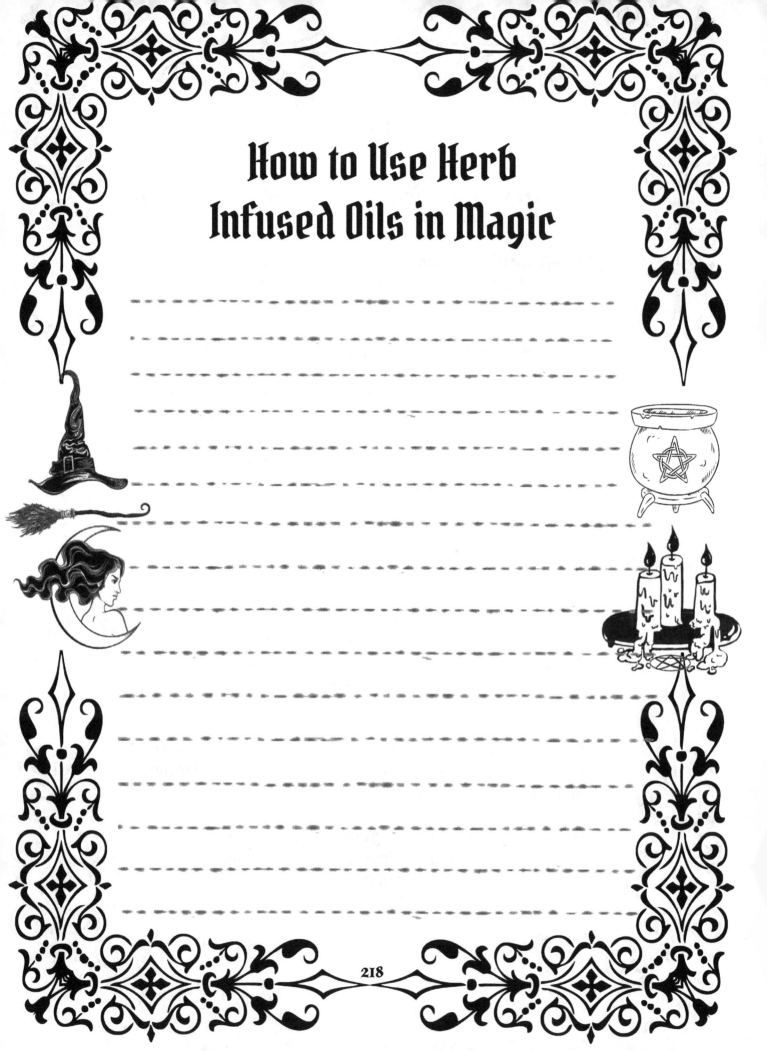

J, H, L

Jasmine: Jasmine is an uplifting oil, increasing love and passion, boosting both physical and mental potency. Ltdeflects potential hostility, modifying it into friendship and a willingness to compromise. It is mixed with most other oils, especially ylang-ylang and rose.

Honeysuckle: Honeysuckle's pleasant scent is ideal for lightening a room. The scent is an excellent aid to intuition and psychic insight. It is used in rituals for love, protection, fidelity, money, supernatural power, and telepathy.

Lilac: Using lilac in rituals or to scent a room, brings harmony and peace to your everyday life. It is soothing and good for protection and warding off negative energies.

Lavender: Lavender is harmonizing oil, brings kindness, love, and reconciliation to any place or person. It mixes well with practically every oil, especially Marjoram, Geranium, Chamomile, ylang-ylang.

Lemon: Lemon is the breath of life, bringing energy, logic, integrity, and clarity. It is a light - bringer, cutting through mystery, doubt and dishonesty, and cleansing atmospheres and attitudes. It mixes well with Eucalyptus, Chamomile, lavender, and myrrh.

Lemongrass: Lemongrass will remove negative emotions among family, friends, and colleagues. It past anger and feuds from the past that no longer serve you. It removes painful memories and helps to leave behind toxic relationships. Lemongrass also enhances psychic awareness. It mixes well with geranium and frankincense.

How to Use Herb Infused Oils in Magic

L - M - N

Lime: Lime brings health and wellbeing to you, your family, and your home. It creates enthusiasm and triggers self-healing and regeneration in your mind and body. It is protective against mental and psychic attacks and has natural therapeutic powers. A citrus oil mixes well with lavender & Eucalyptus.

Mandarin: Mandarin oil restores self-esteem, self-love, and confidence, offers protection against the barbs of unfair criticism, gossip, and spite. It enhances inner beauty and radiance. A citrus oil, it mixes well with ylang-ylang, Cedarwood, and Geranium.

Marjoram: Marjoram relieves the sense of isolation and alienation, loneliness, and awakens empathy with others. It is an oil of enduring fidelity and love. It mixes well with Rosemary and Lavender.

Mimosa: Mimosa is an oil of the night for secret love and secrets, bringing love and friendship, particularly for the elderly. It soothes anxiety and oversensitivity to criticism and brings happiness and harmony, melting away hostility and opposition.
It mixes well with Chamomile and bergamot.

Myrrh: This is pure ceremonial oil, like frankincense, and is burned in purification and healing rituals.
It mixes well with patchouli, mandarin, and pine oil.

Neroli: This is orange-blossom oil, a symbol of fidelity, fertility, marriage, committed relationships, sensuality, and self-esteem. It prevents crises of confidence, mood swings, and panic attacks. It mixes well with jasmine and geranium.

How to Use Herb Infused Oils in Magic

O · P · R

Orange: Orange is the oil of fertility, abundance, confidence, joy, attracting happiness, individuality, calming anxiety, and restlessness in adults and children. It mixes well with Lavender and Ylang-ylang.

Patchouli: Patchouli is the oil of accomplishment and is used mainly in money rituals. It brings employment and enhances business opportunities. It is also generally used in ceremonies to heal the planet and restore balance naturally. It mixes well with myrrh, geranium, and pine.

Peppermint: Peppermint attracts money and offers protection against accidents, illness, hostility, theft, or damage to the home. It mixes well with Eucalyptus.

Pine: Pine protects primarily against emotional blackmail. It is a purifier of all forms of negativity, hostile atmospheres, and dishonesty. It is perseverance under adversity, oil of courage, integrity, and clear focus. It mixes well with marjoram, juniper, and lemon.

Rose: This is an oil of partnerships, fidelity, happiness, gentle healing, love, and particularly self-love. It mixes well with practically every oil.

Rosemary: Rosemary is oil for concentration, enhanced memory, justice, career, and success. It blends with Geranium, Cedarwood &. Frankincense.

Rosewood: Rosewood calms mind, body, and soul, creating a setting helpful to peace at home or work, mainly if there are difficult negotiations, or potentially unfriendly visitors or phone calls. It will also clear away existing conflict. Rosewood soothes restless or hyperactive kids. For adults, it brings acceptance of life as it is. It is suitable for energizing all forms of magic. Rosewood mixes well with geranium, jasmine, and neroli.

How to Use Herb Infused Oils in Magic

S, T, Y

Sandalwood: Sandalwood is oil of sensuality and passion. It emphasizes meditative abilities and increases spiritual awareness. Sandalwood is offering a path to make contact with the higher self, angelic, or spirit guides. It blends very well with many other oils, especially Rosemary, Chamomile, Patchouli, and Lemon.

Tea tree: Tea tree oil is invaluable for absent healing. It will banish negativity, remove blockages in energy, replacing it with optimism, and channeling uneasiness into positive aspects of life. It is usually best used alone but can be mixed with sandalwood only.

Ylang-ylang: The oil of poets, ylang-ylang, is associated with love and inspiration, particularly self-esteem. It prevents a sense of frustration when things cannot be achieved or changed. It increases confidence and pleasure in possibilities that can be realized within the boundaries of your present circumstance. It mixes well with Chamomile, Clary sage, geranium, and lemon.

Magical Oils Recipes

Magical Oil Recipes

Blessing Oil

To make Blessing Oil, use 1/8 Cup base oil of your choice. Add the following:
- 5 drops Sandalwood
- 2 drops Camphor
- 1 drop Orange
- 1 drop Patchouli

As you blend the oils, visualize your intent, and take in the aroma. Know that this oil is sacred and magical. Label, date, and store in a cool, dark place.

Protection Oil

To make Protection Oil, use 1/8 Cup base oil of your choice. Add the following:
- 4 drops Patchouli
- 3 drops Lavender
- 1 drop Mugwort
- 1 drop Hyssop

As you blend the oils, visualize your intent, and take in the aroma. Know that this oil is sacred and magical. Label, date, and store in a cool, dark place.
Use Protection Oil to anoint yourself and those in your home. It will help keep you safe from psychic or magical attacks.

<u>Source</u>: https://www.learnreligions.com/

Magical Oils Recipes

Magical Oil Recipes

Gratitude Oil

To make Gratitude Oil, use 1/8 Cup base oil of your choice. Add the following:
- 5 drops Rose
- 2 drops Vetiver
- 1 drop Agrimony
- A pinch of ground cinnamon

Label, date, and store in a cool, dark place.

Money Oil

To make Money Oil, use 1/8 Cup base oil of your choice. Add the following:
- 5 drops Sandalwood
- 5 drops Patchouli
- 2 drops Ginger
- 2 drops Vetiver
- 1 drop Orange

As you blend the oils, visualize your intent, and take in the aroma. Label, date, and store in a cool, dark place.

Source: https://www.learnreligions.com

Magical Oils Recipes

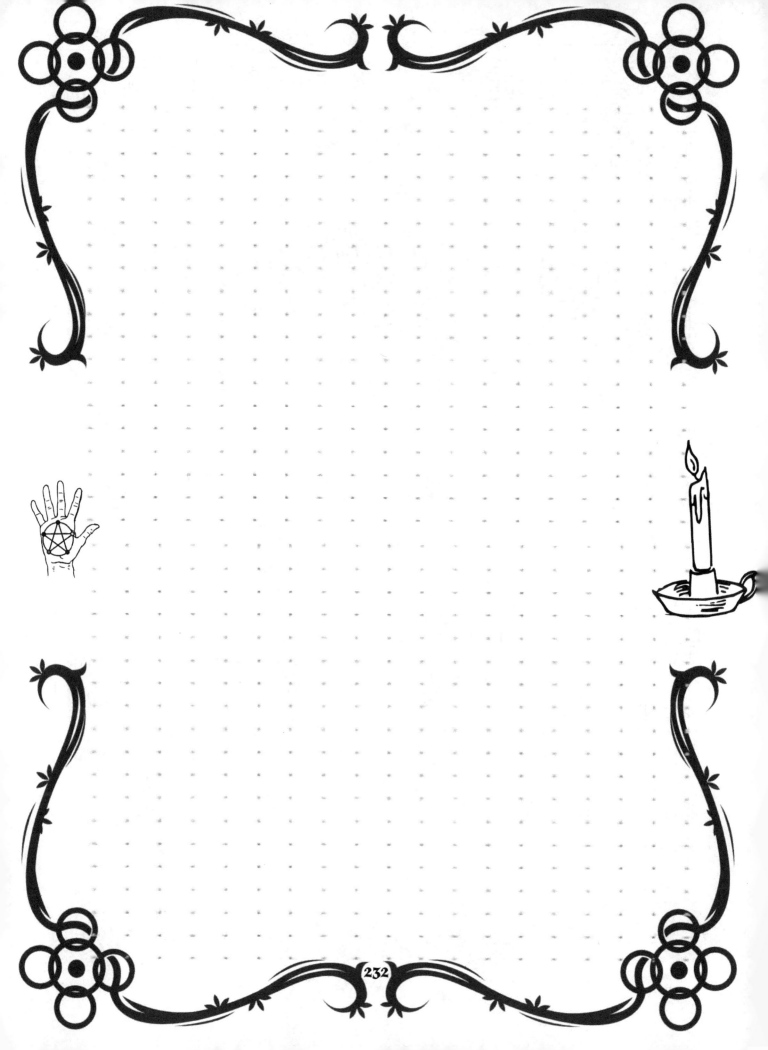

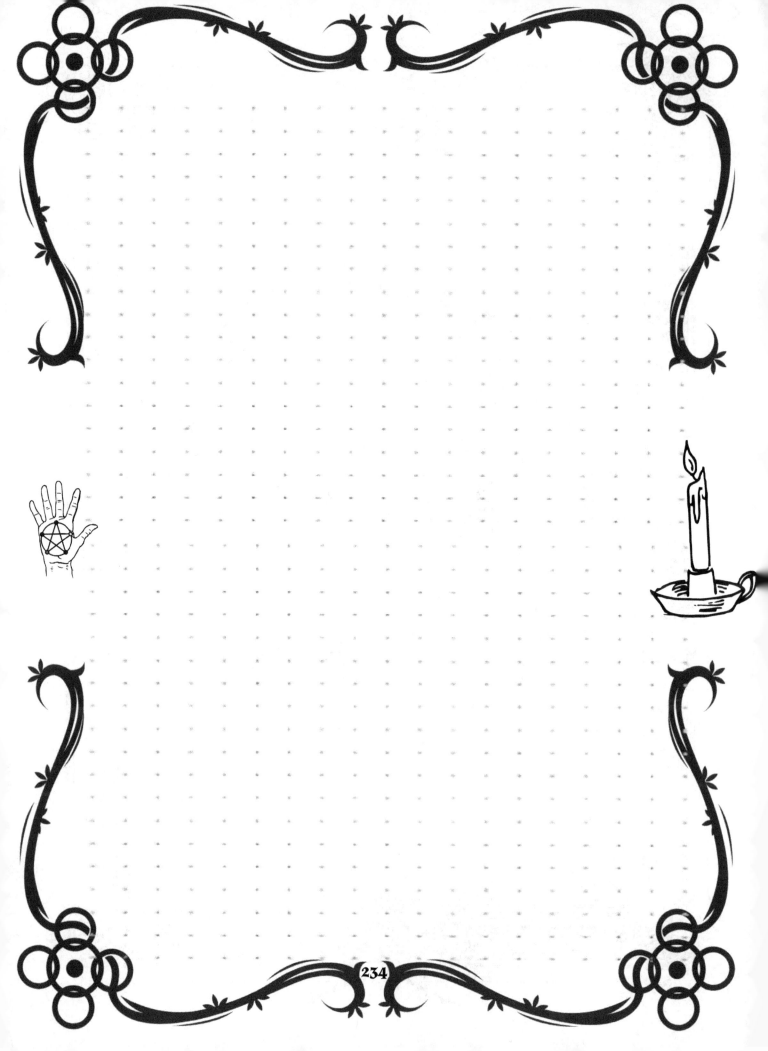

Signs of a Spell Working

My Feelings & Emotions

Coincidences:

Dreams:

New Opportunities:

Indirect Indicators:

Increased Contact:

Signs of a Spell Working

My Feelings & Emotions

_____
_____
_____
_____
_____
_____

Coincidences:

_____
_____
_____
_____
_____
_____

Dreams:

_____
_____
_____
_____
_____
_____
_____

New Opportunities:

_____
_____
_____
_____
_____
_____

Indirect Indicators:

_____
_____
_____
_____
_____

Increased Contact:

_____
_____
_____
_____
_____

My Spell

Here is a simple, straightforward way to help you be organized and have all your information for a spell in one place.

Intent Purpose _____
_____
_____

Date _____ Time _____

Astrological & Planetary Influences _____

Place _____ _____ _____

(significance) _____

Space set up _____
_____

Grounding Technique _____

Call Corners _____

Divine _____

Tools
_____
_____
_____
_____
_____
_____
_____
_____
_____
_____

Dress
_____
_____
_____
_____
_____
_____
_____
_____
_____
_____
_____

Words of Power

_____
_____
_____
_____

Method to raise energy _____ Release _____

Offerings & Gratitude _____
_____

Open circle _____

After Spell Action _____
_____
_____

Result:

Magical Color Correspondences

Black	Addictions, Bad Habits, Banishing, Binding, Confusion, Decisions, Discord, Protection, Remove Hexes, Spirit Contact, Truth, Ward Negativity
Blue	Art, Changes, Employment, Happiness, Harmony, Health
Brown	Animal Health, Balance, Concentration, Earth Elemental, Empathy, Endurance, ESP, Foundations, Grounding, Houses, Physical Objects, Steadiness, Uncertainties
Copper	Monetary goals, Passion, Professional growth
Dark Blue	Change, Dreams, Impulse, Meditation, Protection, The Goddess, Truth, Water
Emerald Green	Fertility, Love
Gold	Abundance, Achievement, Business, Divination, Employment, Finances, Fortune, Healing Energy, Intuition, Mental Growth, Physical Strength, Power, Skill, Solar Energy, Success, The God
Green	Abundance, Agriculture, Agriculture, Ambition, Balance, Changing direction, Courage, Earth Elemental, Employment, Fertility, Finances, Generosity, Greed, Growth, Habits, Healing, Herb Magick, Lord and Lady, Luck, Prosperity
Green-Yellow	Anger, Jealousy, Negate Discord, Sickness
Grey	Cancellation, Decisions, Faerie Magick, Hesitation, Neutrality, Vision Quests
Indigo	Astral Work, Balance, Competition, Defense, Gossip, Karma Workings, Meditation, Neutralise Magic, Spirit Communication, Ward Slander
Lavender	Dignity, Intuition, Spiritual shield
Light Blue	Intuition, Opportunity, Patience, Psychic Awareness, Quests, Safe Journey, Tranquility, Understanding, Ward depression
Olive green	Forgiveness
Orange	Adaptability, Attraction, Changes, Control, Dominance, Employment, The God, Encouragement, Energy, Healing, Legal Matters, Luck, Strength, Vitality
Peach	Gentle strength, Joy
Pink	Affection, Awakening, Communication, Compassion, Emotional Love, Friendship, Honour, Mortality, Relaxation
Purple	Ambition, Banish Disease, Banish Evil, Business, Healing, Intuition, Meditation, Occult Wisdom, Power, Progress, Protection, Spiritual Communication, Spiritual Development
Red	Adaptability, Bad Habits, Banishing, Courage, Defense, Energy, Enthusiasm, Fear, Fire Elemental, Habits, Health, Passion, Power, Protection, Sexuality, Strength, Vigor
Silver	Abundance, Balance, Fear, Lunar Magic, Meditation, Psychic Development, Success, The Goddess, Ward Negativity
Turquoise	Growth, Healing, Peace, Prosperity
Violet	Addictions, Intuition, Self-Improvement, Success
White	Acceptance, Banishing, Blessing, Clairvoyance, Clarity, Consecration, Decisions, Devotions, Forgiveness, Full Moon Magic, Harmony, Justice, Meditation, Peace, Protection, Purity, Sincerity, Truth, Warding
Yellow	Adaptability, Air Elemental, Art, Attraction, Changes, Clairvoyance, Study, Travel, Communication, Concentration, Confidence, Creativity, Divination, Eloquence, Fertility, Harmony, Intellectual Growth, Learning, Mental Alertness, Prosperity

My Spell

Here is a simple, straightforward way to help you be organized and have all your information for a spell in one place.

Intent Purpose _____
_____
_____

Date _____ Time _____

Astrological & Planetary Influences _____

Place _____ _____ _____

(significance) _____

Space set up _____
_____

Grounding Technique _____

Call Corners _____

Divine _____

Tools
_____
_____
_____
_____
_____
_____
_____
_____
_____

Dress
_____
_____
_____
_____
_____
_____
_____
_____
_____
_____
_____

Words of Power

_____
_____
_____
_____
_____

Method to raise energy _____ Release _____

Offerings & Gratitude _____
_____

Open circle _____

After Spell Action _____
_____

Result:

My Recipes

My Recipes

My Favorite Magic Books

Scents, essential oils and incense recipes

My Spell

Here is a simple, straightforward way to help you be organized and have all your information for a spell in one place.

Intent Purpose _____
_____
_____

Date _____ Time _____

Astrological & Planetary Influences _____

Place _____ _____

(significance) _____

Space set up _____
_____

Grounding Technique _____

Call Corners _____

Divine _____

Tools
_____
_____
_____
_____
_____
_____
_____

Dress
_____
_____
_____
_____
_____
_____
_____
_____

Words of Power

_____
_____
_____
_____

Method to raise energy_____ Release _____

Offerings & Gratitude _____
_____

Open circle_____

After Spell Action _____
_____
_____

Result:

My Notes

Signs That my Magic is Manifesting and Working

Notes

My Spell

Here is a simple, straightforward way to help you be organized and have all your information for a spell in one place.

Intent Purpose _____

_____

_____

Date _____ Time _____

Astrological & Planetary Influences _____

Place _____ _____

(significance) _____

Space set up _____

_____

Grounding Technique _____

Call Corners _____

Divine _____

Tools
_____
_____
_____
_____
_____
_____
_____
_____
_____
_____
Dress
_____
_____
_____
_____
_____
_____
_____
_____
_____
_____

Words of Power

_____

_____

_____

_____

_____

Method to raise energy _____ Release _____

Offerings & Gratitude _____

_____

Open circle _____

After Spell Action _____

_____

_____

Result:

My Spell

Here is a simple, straightforward way to help you be organized and have all your information for a spell in one place.

Intent Purpose _____
_____
_____

Date _____ Time _____

Astrological & Planetary Influences _____

Place _____ _____ _____
(significance) _____
Space set up_____
_____
Grounding Technique_____

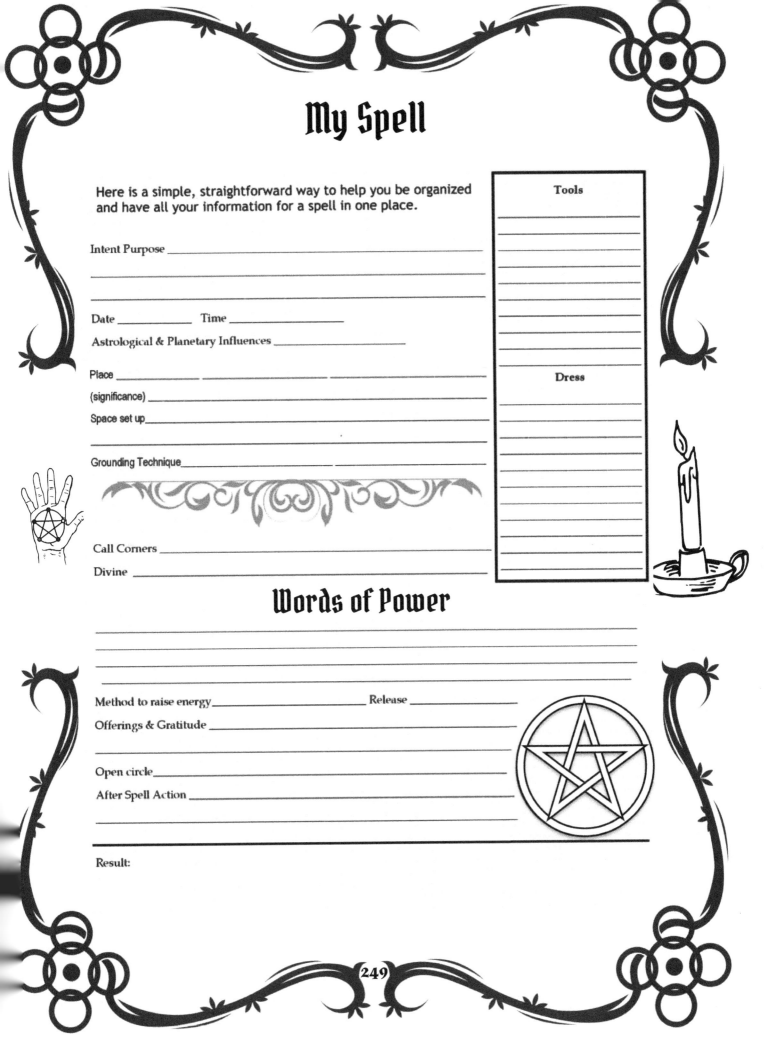

Call Corners _____
Divine _____

Tools
_____
_____
_____
_____
_____
_____
_____
_____

Dress
_____
_____
_____
_____
_____
_____
_____
_____
_____
_____
_____

Words of Power

_____
_____
_____
_____

Method to raise energy_____ Release _____
Offerings & Gratitude _____
_____
Open circle_____
After Spell Action _____
_____
_____

Result:

My Path to Magic

Notes

Add to your collection more Book of Shadows for Coloring.
Check them on YouTube before enjoying your paper copy.

Flip Through:

The Wiccan Sabbats, Candle Color Meanings, Healing Herbs, Essential Oils, Color & Make Your Own Spells

COLORING BOOK OF SHADOWS VOL 1

http://bit.ly/Vol1BOS

Flip Through:

Wicca Elemental Magic, Planets & Days of the Week. Color & Make Your Own Spells

COLORING BOOK OF SHADOWS VOL 2

http://bit.ly/Vol2BOS

Flip Through:

Zodiac Signs Magic Powers, Compatibility, Correspondences & Abilities of Each Sign

COLORING BOOK OF SHADOWS VOL 3

http://bit.ly/Vol3bos

My YouTube Channel
http://bit.ly/YouTubeWicca

Blessed Be!

Resources

Visit our Etsy shop for more BOS pages:

https://www.etsy.com/shop/WiccaWitchcraft

15% off any order

Apply coupon: **FAVORITE** on the checkout

Websites used for research:

https://ayearandadaywicca.wordpress.com
https://www.learnreligions.com
https://www.johnhuntpublishing.com
https://www.groveandgrotto.com
https://thenewpagan.wordpress.com
https://witchcraft-wicca.com/
https://www.shutterstock.com
http://www.thewhitegoddess.co.uk
https://witcheslore.com
https://www.tumblr.com/
https://www.johnhuntpublishing.com
https://plentifulearth.com/
https://lightwarriorslegion.com/

Blessed Be!

CPSIA information can be obtained
at www.ICGtesting.com
Printed in the USA
LVHW061147040421
683394LV00007B/407